CONTENTS

Helion & Company Limited
Unit 8 Amherst Business Centre, Budbrooke Road, Warwick CV34 5WE, England
Tel. 01926 499 619
Fax 0121 711 4075
Email: info@helion.co.uk   Website: www.helion.co.uk   Twitter: @helionbooks   Visit our blog http://blog.helion.co.uk/

Published by Helion & Company 2019
Designed and typeset by Farr out Publications, Wokingham, Berkshire
Cover designed by Paul Hewitt, Battlefield Design (www.battlefield-design.co.uk)
Printed by Henry Ling Ltd, Dorchester, Dorset

Text and maps © Athol Yates & Cliff Lord 2019
Photographs © as individually credited
Colour profiles © Tom Cooper, David Bocquelet and Anderson Subtil 2019

All names, locations and geographic designations are those used in the UAE today, where Arabic words are invariably transliterated,
rather than transcripted. This practice was introduced because of the large number of non-Arabic speakers living in the country.

Cover: A Saracen armoured personnel carrier of the ADDF in the early 1970s (photo courtesy of Alistair MacDonald) and
a Hawker Hunter FGA.Mk 76 of the ADDF's Air Wing of the same period (artwork profile by Tom Cooper).

ISBN 978-1-912390-61-8

British Library Cataloguing-in-Publication Data.
A catalogue record for this book is available from the British Library.

For details of other military history titles published by Helion & Company Limited contact the above address, or visit our
website: http://www.helion.co.uk. We always welcome receiving book proposals from prospective authors.

ABBREVIATIONS

2IC	second-in-command
AA	anti-aircraft
AD	air defence
ADDF	Abu Dhabi Defence Force
agal	camel hobble worn on top of the *shemagh*
AML	Auto Mitrailleuse Légère (light armoured car)
AMX-30	French main battle tank
APC	armoured personnel carrier
Armd	armoured
BDE	brigade
Bn	battalion
Bty	battery
chaplis	sandals
CID	Criminal Investigation Department
C-in-C	Commander-in-Chief
CMC	Central Military Command
CO	Commanding Officer
COMTOS	Commander Trucial Oman Scouts
Coy	company
DDF	Dubai Defence Force
dhow	Traditional Gulf Arabic vessel
DIO	Desert Intelligence Officer
est.	established
FAC	fast attack craft (vessel)
FAF	Federal Armed Forces
FCO	Foreign and Commonwealth Office (UK)
Fd	field
FFR	Fitted for Radio
FHQ	Force Headquarters
FIO	Field Intelligence Officer
FO	Foreign Office (UK)
FPB	fast patrol boat
GHQ	general headquarters
GSO	General Staff Office
HOW	howitzer
HQ	headquarters
Inf	Infantry
khunjah	dagger (Gulf States)
LAA	light anti-aircraft
LAD	light aid detachment
LFPG	Land Forces Persian Gulf (UK)
LMG	light machine gun
LSO	Loan Service Officer
LWB	long wheel-base
mazri	cotton material
MMG	medium machine gun
MoD	Ministry of Defence
MoU	memorandum of understanding
MT	motor transport
na	not applicable
NCO	non-commissioned officer
OC	officer commanding
OR	Other Ranks
PFLOAG	Popular Front for the Liberation of Oman and the Arabian Gulf
puttees	strip of khaki cloth covering the lower part of the leg from the ankle to the knee
QM	quartermaster

r.	ruled
RA	Royal Artillery (UK)
RAC	Royal Armoured Corps (UK)
RAF	Royal Air Force (UK)
RAKMF	Ras Al Khaimah Mobile Force
RAOC	Royal Army Ordnance Corps (UK)
RCL	recoilless rifle
RCT	Royal Corps of Transport (UK)
RE	Royal Engineers (UK)
recce	reconnaissance
REME	Royal Electrical and Mechanical Engineers (UK)
Rgt	Regiment
RPC	Royal Pioneer Corps (UK)
RSigs	Royal Signals (UK)
RSM	Regimental Sergeant Major
sabkha	salt flat
SAS	Special Air Service (UK)
shemagh	Arab cloth headdress worn with or without an *agal*
Sigcen	Signal Centre
SLR	self-loading rifle
SNG	Sharjah National Guard
SO	Staff Officer
SP	self propelled
SpGp	Support Group
SQN	squadron
STOL	short take-off and landing
TAC Sign	coloured sign on front and rear of vehicles denoting regiment or service
TNA	The National Archives (UK)
TOL	Trucial Oman Levies
TOS	Trucial Oman Scouts
TOW	tube-launched, optically tracked, wire-guided (US-made anti-tank missile)
Tp	troop
Trg	training
UAE	United Arab Emirates
UAQNG	Umm Al Quwain National Guard
UDF	Union Defence Force
UK	United Kingdom
US	United States
wadi	a valley
WAM	Emirates News Agency
WO	Warrant Officer

1

THE EMIRATES

The UAE is a federation comprising seven emirates–Abu Dhabi, Ajman, Dubai, Fujairah, Ras Al Khaimah, Sharjah and Umm Al Quwain. Each is headed by a Ruler, which is effectively a hereditary post held by a member of that Emirate's Ruling Family. The UAE was formed in 1971, with the Emirates previously being collectively known as the Trucial States. The UAE is about the size of Scotland with a mainland area of around 77,700 km². It is situated in the Lower Gulf region and has coastlines in both the Arabian Gulf and the Gulf of Oman.

The Arabian Gulf is a relatively shallow body of water with a depth that rarely exceeds 90m. Historically, the Gulf has been valued for its fishing and pearl oysters, and as a route for transporting goods and people. From the early 20th century, it has been globally critical

Figure 1: The Arabian Peninsula and region

as a key route for the transport of oil and gas.

At around 400km east to west and 350km north to south, the UAF's mainland areas provide no strategic depth to which its military could retreat and regroup following any large-scale attack (see Figure 1). The country's vulnerability is compounded by its small population (which in 1968 was just 180,000), and the concentration of government, population and economic activity in just a few large cities on the Arabian Gulf coast, with smaller concentrations on the East Coast, notably Fujairah and Khor Fakkan.

The UAE neighbours four countries – Qatar, Oman, Saudi Arabia and Iran. Over the period from 1951 to 1980, all four disputed their territorial or maritime boundaries with the Emirates, and these tensions significantly drove the development of the security forces in the Emirates. The dispute with Qatar involved the ownership of land and islands in Abu Dhabi's far west as at that time, the two states shared a border. This dispute ended in the 1960s when Britain, which was then responsible for the external affairs of all Lower Gulf states, unilaterally decided the location of the borders. Disputes with Oman waxed and waned over the decades, with the major ones relevant to this book being over the border location in the area of the inland Buraimi Oasis, adjacent to the Abu Dhabi

town of Al Ain, and eastern areas including with Ras Al Khaimah in its north, with Dubai in the area of Hatta, and with Sharjah and Fujairah over the size of the Omani Madhah enclave inside UAE territory. It was only in 2002 that a final agreement on the roughly 1,000km common border between the two countries was signed.

The territorial dispute with Saudi Arabia has its origins in the arrival of a Wahhabi force in the area in the 1800s. This provided Saudi Arabia with a justification in 1949 to unilaterally declare a new border line, claiming some 80 percent of the onshore territory of Abu Dhabi and large parts of Oman. The Saudi claim included the Al Ain/Buraimi Oases as it could provide them with a base from which to extend their influence into both Oman and Abu Dhabi. At that time, the oases had a population of some 25,000 spread over nine villages. Six of these were governed by Abu Dhabi's Ruler and three by the Sultan of Oman. Britain, Abu Dhabi and Oman rejected Saudi Arabia's claim and sought negotiations. To press its claim, in August 1952 a small Saudi force occupied Hamasa, one of the Omani villages in Buraimi. The Saudis remained until 1955 when the British forcefully evicted them with the support of Abu Dhabi and local forces. Britain immediately and unilaterally declared a new border between Abu Dhabi and Saudi Arabia.

Table 1: Key characteristics of the Emirates

Emirate or country	Capital city	Ruling Family (Tribe if the family is a section of a tribe)	Resident population, 1968 numbers / (% of Emirates population)	Mainland area km² / (% of total UAE mainland area)	Proven oil reserves billion barrels / (% of UAE reserves)
Abu Dhabi	Abu Dhabi	Al Nahyan (Bani Yas)	46,375 (26%)	67,340 (87%)	92.2 (93.9%)
Dubai	Dubai	Al Maktoum (Bani Yas)	58,971 (33%)	3,885 (5%)	4 (4.1%)
Sharjah	Sharjah	Al Qasimi	31,668 (18%)	2,590 (3%)	1.5 (1.5%)
Ras Al Khaimah	Ras Al Khaimah	Al Qasimi	24,387 (14%)	1,684 (2%)	
Fujairah	Fujairah	Al Sharqiyyin	9,735 (5%)	1,165 (1.5%)	
Ajman	Ajman	Al Na'im	4,246 (2%)	259 (0.3%)	0 0
Umm Al Quwain	Umm Al Quwain	Al Mu'alla (Al Ali)	3,744 (2%)	777 (1%)	0 0
UAE	Abu Dhabi		180,226	77,700	97.8

The new border was not accepted by Saudi Arabia, but it did not press its claim again until the late 1960s when Britain's departure from the Gulf was apparent. Saudi Arabia made its diplomatic recognition of the UAE contingent on a suitable settlement, as well threatening to revert to its proclaimed 1949 border if a suitable settlement was not achieved. Recognising the political difficulties of an ongoing disagreement with its largest neighbour, in 1974 Sheikh Zayed reluctantly signed the Treaty of Jeddah to settle the dispute. This gave Saudi Arabia ownership of land covering some 80 percent of the giant Zarrarah oil field (known as the Shaybah oil field by Saudi Arabia), and a 25km-wide corridor of land near Khor Al Odaid in Abu Dhabi's far west which cut the land connection between Abu Dhabi and Qatar. The agreement left the whole of the Buraimi/Al Ain area as part of Oman and Abu Dhabi.

The territorial dispute with Iran, which is still ongoing, involves Iran's occupation of three islands – Abu Musa which is owned by Sharjah, and Greater Tunb and Lesser Tunb which are owned by Ras Al Khaimah. Iran's annexation of the Tunb islands occurred on 30 November 1971, one day before Britain ended its protection of the Emirates. A Ras Al Khaimah policeman was killed during Iran's invasion. British military forces did not respond to Iran's action, and the police and military forces of Ras Al Khaimah were too small to mount an effective challenge. The island of Abu Musa was taken over in 1971 by Iran and has been used as a military base since 1992.

The Emirates are in effect city-states, with their capitals carrying the same name as the Emirate. Most of the population of each Emirate lives in their capital. Abu Dhabi is the capital of the UAE. There are considerable differences in the size, geography, population and resources of each Emirate. As seen in Table 1, Abu Dhabi has the largest territory, is the most populous and owns the vast bulk of all oil in the UAE.

An unusual feature of the UAE are its internal borders. Several Emirates have enclaves within other Emirates and this reflects historic arrangements under which the extent of a Ruler's domain was primarily governed by the land grazed or owned by the tribes that gave allegiance to that Ruler. Thus the Ruler's domain changed over time to reflect changes in both tribal allegiances and the tribes' location, size, power and prestige. In the 1950s, the boundaries between each Emirate were formally agreed to by the Rulers based on tribal allegiance. This resulted in enclaves being formed within other Emirates. In a small number of locations, the tribal boundaries and hence the Emirate borders were unresolved and a frequent cause of inter-Emirate tension and tribal conflict. These unresolved conflicts were another key driver in the shaping of the security forces in the Emirates. One common way to calm tensions was to locate police/military posts or even bases in trouble spots. Examples of this are the military bases established in the 1970s at Masafi and Khor Fakkan.

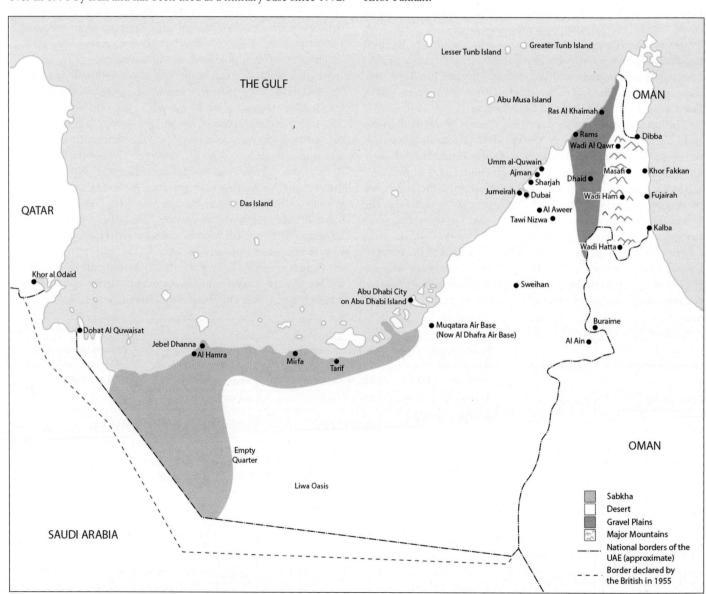

Figure 2: Geography and key locations in the UAE to 1980

THE PHYSICAL ENVIRONMENT

The UAE can be divided into four topographical zones: (1) The coastal plain and *sabkha* of the Arabian Gulf coast. *Sabkha* is salt-encrusted, low-lying mud-like flats that exist in areas where the heavily-saline water table is close to the surface. It is firm when dry, but after rain the crust impedes drainage with the result that the *sabkha* turns into a quagmire which is impractical to cross. (2) The desert. Sand desert dominates most of the south and west of the UAE, and merges into the Empty Quarter (Rub Al Khali) which spans the emirate of Abu Dhabi and Saudi Arabia and is the largest sand desert in the world, with inter-dunal *sabkha* in places. Dunes can reach 300 metres in height with up to a 50-degree slipface, making travel difficult. Given the arid environment, permanent settlement was only possible in two areas which had reliable groundwater–the Liwa and Al Ain/Buraimi Oases. (3) The steep and rugged Hajar Mountains, a 65km long and 25km wide mountain chain in the UAE's east. The mountains plunge into the sea along much of the coast of the Gulf of Oman, creating steep cliffs which cannot be ascended from the sea. There are only a few sandy beaches and small natural harbours along this coast. There are relatively narrow coastal plains which are the outwash plains from major wadis that offer routes through the mountains, such as Wadi Ham. In these areas, small settlements existed, such as Dibba, Fujairah and Kalba. (4) The narrow fertile alluvial gravel plains. These are to the west of the Hajar Mountains, and movement across these plains is relatively easy.

Before the advent of motor vehicles, most people who travelled from Abu Dhabi to the Oman coast travelled via the Al Ain/Buraimi Oases. People travelling from Qatar/Saudi Arabia to Abu Dhabi had two main routes – by vessel and along the coast. To get to the Al Ain/Buraimi Oases from Saudi Arabia, a less well travelled route was across the Empty Quarter south of Liwa. People travelling from the East Coast towns like Fujairah and Dibba could travel across narrow mountain tracks to the Arabian Gulf towns. Control of these routes was thus essential to protecting the Emirates. This explains why the British military and Emirati military and police forces placed great importance on monitoring and controlling these routes. Unsurprisingly, the first military posts in the Trucial States were located along these routes (e.g. at Tarif, Wadi Al Qawr and Al Ain).

The climate of the Emirates is harsh, since the country is in the subtropical arid zone of the Middle East. Its average annual rainfall is very low although there is considerable variation across the country. Typically, average annual rainfall is 78mm a year, but far less falls in the south-west desert areas. The summers are very hot, reaching 50°C with 100 percent humidity. There are no permanent rivers or lakes in the UAE, with only a few permanent springs in the mountains, notably in the Hajar Mountains of Fujairah. This meant that virtually all water came from ground sources, wells or from systems built to catch winter rainfall, until desalination became viable. There was also the transport of water from elsewhere, such as from Kuwait or Al Ain. There are two main seasons – winter (December to March) and summer (June to September) – which are separated by two short transition periods.

THE PEOPLE

The Emirates' barren environment resulted in the evolution of two distinct types of traditional lifestyles: nomadic (*bedu*) and settled (*hadhr*) Arabs.

The *bedu* moved constantly in search of grazing for their camels and goats, and in the Emirates typically moved in winter towards the coast, and in the summer to the cooler oases. While some *bedu* travelled continuously, many were semi-nomadic in that they regularly returned to a permanent settlement. The *bedu* earned income through the sale of camels and their products, by transporting people and goods across the deserts, by providing security for desert caravans, and by undertaking seasonal employment like manning the pearling boats which went to sea over summer. As *bedu* could raid settlements and provide protection from other raiders, some *bedu* tribes collected tribute from settled groups in return for security.

Rather than being powerless in the face of the *bedu*, settled Arabs could exert power over nomadic groups by controlling access to water and other vital resources, as well as creating rivalry between *bedu* groups through the ability to make loyalty payments, alliances with external powers and other tactics. The prominent section/tribe of a settled group would generally seek to establish alliances with *bedu* groups for mutual advantage. These could result in a symbiotic partnership which enabled a settled group to dominate a region politically and militarily.

In the Emirates, most *hadhr* lived on the coast, undertaking pearling, fishing, maritime trade, boat building, craft work, or cultivation or animal husbandry either in mountains of the northern Emirates or oases of Abu Dhabi and other townships like Dhaid in Sharjah, and Khatt in Ras Al Khaimah. Like the *bedu*, some would migrate to the coast in winter to trade or work, and return inland for summer.

In terms of numbers, the *bedu* have always been outnumbered by settled Arabs. Despite their smaller number, the *bedu* controlled the deserts of the region and only through negotiating with them could one cross or use their land. As the *bedu* represented both a threat and source of protection for settlements, their importance in local politics was disproportionate to their number. With the introduction of modern weapons, wireless, automobiles and aircraft into the interior of the Emirates, which started in earnest in the 1950s, the power and influence of the *bedu* started to decline. No longer were the *bedu* the gatekeepers to the desert, nor could they use it as a refuge from which to launch raids. Vehicles meant that camels had little transport value, and the work of *bedu* as guides for travellers and oil company seismic teams ended with the building of major tracks and roads. By the late 1960s, the traditional *bedu* life was no longer sustainable and they were increasingly settled in new townships or on farms in the interior.

In addition to the Arab *hadhr*, the coastal towns were home to communities of geographical Persian origin and Indian trading families. The former group were mainly of Arab ethnicity but some were ethnic Persians. The vast majority of Emiratis belong to the Sunni sect of Islam, however a small percentage are Shia. Some Indian trading families were Hindus and some Khojas (Ismailis). Unlike neighbouring states like Oman, Bahrain and Saudi Arabia, the Emirates have avoided deep-seated sectarian disputes due to a combination of a small number of non-Sunnis, and the Rulers' tolerance of other sects and religions. Consequently, the Iranian leadership's called to Muslims, and Shias in particular, to rise up and overthrow the Gulf monarchs following the 1979 Islamic revolution failed to resonate in the Emirates.

Rather than religion, the ideological threats to stability in the Emirates came from revolutionary beliefs, notably pan-Arabism, Nasserism, Baathism and communism. While the Emirates avoided revolutionary civil wars such as occurred in Oman, a key concern was to prevent these conflicts from spilling over into the Emirates, and to prevent revolutionary cells from subverting the population and government. Targeting these groups has been an enduring priority for both military intelligence and Police Special Branches.

A defining element of Emirati society is its tribal heritage, which has shaped both the political system and the security services. (Note a significant number of Emirati families in coastal settlements fall outside the tribal system – these are often families of Persian, but ethnic Arab, origin.)

A tribe is a collection of families linked by the notion of both kinship to a common male ancestor, and loyalty. Integral to this definition are concepts of the family, affiliation and heritage, as well as the notion of the primacy of the group over individuals in return for reciprocity and protection.

The fundamental social unit in a tribe is the family, which is hierarchical and patriarchal. The central authority figure is the father who is entitled to deference and unquestioning compliance. His role is breadwinner and provider. The oldest brother has this responsibility in the father's absence or death. A family is an exclusive network where membership rests solely on birth. However, qualified entry can occur through marriage and fostership. The family takes precedence over all temporal issues including work, friends and personal desires. Loyalty is to the family, which creates wide-ranging and powerful mutual obligations to family members.

The head of a tribal grouping is a sheikh. The role of the traditional sheikh is described by Edward Henderson, an Arabic-speaking Briton who played a major role in the 1950s Buraimi crisis with Saudi Arabia and served as the British Political Agent in Abu Dhabi from 1959 to 1961, having previously worked for the Iraq Petroleum Company, which, through a subsidiary, held the onshore oil concessions in the Emirates:

> The leader's duties in all tribes are the upholding of religion, attending the Friday prayer, the question of deciding matters of defence, of war and peace, the punishment of wrongdoers, the administration of justice, the collection of taxes (especially the religious tax), the administration of funds and personal supervision of all the community's affairs. He must also have *hadh* (good fortune) – priority is to make peace not war, and protect without violence.

As noted above, a fundamental responsibility of the sheikh is to maintain peace and protection, ideally without violence. In a subsistence economy, conflict can pose an existential threat to a tribe as it diverts resources away from productive activities, and causes property destruction, injury and death. Thus, great value is placed on a leader being able to maintain peace and stability, a challenge made even more difficult by the Arab conception of the world that strife is endemic.

Sheikhs are generally appointed and removed by a council of tribal elders and the sheikh's family members.

A Ruler is the paramount sheikh of the Emirate's dominant tribe. The position of the sheikh and Ruler does not automatically pass from father to son, however it is often dynastic in that it generally only passes to a member of the former Ruler's immediate family. Each Emirate has its own Ruling Family and these families have been the source of the Emirates' Rulers for over 200 years. Table 1 lists the Ruling Families and the tribes from which they come.

Like the Arab family, the tribal structure is patriarchal and hierarchical. This means that decisions are centralised with the sheikhs and Ruler. While decisions are generally made after consultation with tribal elders and notables, the actual decisions are theirs alone. Consequently, they are held personally accountable for both their successes and failures.

The authority of a Ruler stems from a combination of his nobility of lineage, personal influence, wealth, largesse and ability to develop consensus. Over time, through demonstrating sound judgement and knowing the probable consensus in advance, a Ruler becomes the acknowledged authority, with less need to ask for advice from the sheikhs and members of his family. Critical to keeping the support of the tribe is the distribution of largesse where the Ruler provides patronage, gifts, hospitality and payments.

Traditionally, as Rulers had limited income they could not afford a large, standing security force. Instead, they had to rely on a small number of (1) retainers (*mutarizaya*) some of whom were armed, (2) armed guards at the Ruler's forts (*haras*), (3) armed tribesmen paid a salary to enforce the Ruler's authority (*askari*), and (4) armed guards in settlements and outlying regions (*duris*). In times of conflict, the Ruler would mobilise additional men from his own and allied tribes.

The tribal heritage has had a strong influence on Emirati security forces since their inception. This can be seen in the enduring priority given to security by the Rulers, the preference for members of historically loyal tribes to fill sensitive posts, and the militarisation of armed retainers into a Ruler's protection force.

A paramount priority for the Rulers has always been to provide – and to be seen to provide – security and stability within their emirate. This need resulted in all the Rulers with financial means establishing their own militaries (i.e. Abu Dhabi, Dubai, Sharjah, Ras Al Khaimah and Umm Al Quwain). It also meant that most Rulers were reluctant to transfer control of their police and military to the Federal Ministry of Interior and UAE Armed Forces' General Headquarters as this meant a loss of self-protection and prestige. However, even today, nearly all Rulers still maintain some control over the small unit devoted to his own personal security although these are formally part of the overall UAE Armed Forces.

Another continuity with the past has been the high degree of personal control that Rulers have exercised over their security forces. This control was mostly exercised directly or through their oldest and/or most appropriate son, who generally served as the political head of the force with responsibility to oversee the executive head of the force. Reinforcing the Ruler's direct control over the service forces reflects the Arab culture of centralised decision-making with decisions pushed upwards. This has meant that Rulers and their sons were not only involved in all strategic-level decisions, but were also involved in decisions at a level which would typically be delegated to senior officers or bureaucrats in a Western police or military force.

Another tribal pattern that can be seen at least to 1980 relates to the employment of people with tribal heritage linked to the Ruling Family. There has been a preference for filling sensitive posts from tribes who have shown historic loyalty to the Ruler. Sensitive posts are the (1) most senior force commands (e.g. Under-Secretary, Chief of Staff and Commander Air Force), (2) critical operational commanders (e.g. Assistant Chief of Staff Operations, Commander Emiri Guard (i.e. a Ruler's protection force), and Assistant Commandant for Operations) (3) high-readiness units (e.g. Commanders of Special Operations and Riot Police) and (4) intelligence functions (e.g. Directorate of Military Intelligence and Special Branch).

From the late 1960s, the Abu Dhabi Ruler sought to build support across the Emirates for a federated state following the scheduled departure of the British in 1971. Just as historically a sheikh would build support by paying tribes in return for allegiance, the recruiting of Emiratis from other Emirates into the Federal Ministry of the Interior and UAE Armed Forces can be seen as a continuation of this approach. Serving as a soldier or policeman was particularly important for those from the northern Emirates of Ajman, Umm Al

Quwain, Ras Al Khaimah and Fujairah due to a lack of employment opportunities in those areas. It not only generated individual income for the family, it in effect aligned the interests of the northern tribes with the success of federation. This explains the disproportionally large number of security force members from the northern Emirates that has always existed in the UAE security forces.

OIL CHANGED EVERYTHING

The discovery of oil in the late 1950s fundamentally changed the characteristics of the Trucial States. Within a few decades, the region went from an undeveloped, subsistence and illiterate society to an advanced emerging market economy, and today the UAE has one of the world's greatest levels of per capita income.

Commercial oil deposits were first discovered in the emirates in 1958, long after oil had been discovered in the other countries surrounding the Arabian Gulf. This meant that all the other countries had much greater levels of development than the Trucial States which, at that time, had very few schools and hospitals, and no paved roads, piped water or electricity. In 1962, the first oil exports were shipped from Abu Dhabi's Das Island, and this saw a massive increase in revenues for the Abu Dhabi Ruler. Subsequent oil fields were discovered across Abu Dhabi, both on and off shore. Commercial quantities of oil were found in Dubai Emirate in 1966 with exports starting three years later, and Sharjah in 1972 with exports starting two years later.

The oil and gas reserves of the UAE are massive. Currently the UAE has around 7 percent of the world's oil and 3 percent of the world's gas reserves. As seen in Table 1, Abu Dhabi possesses nearly 94 percent of the UAE's oil, with Dubai having 4.1 percent, Sharjah 1.5 percent and Ras Al Khaimah having 0.5 percent. No commercial oil or gas fields have been identified in the other Emirates. Protecting oil production facilities and oil-rich land/territorial waters from annexation has been an enduring driver of the Emirates' security services.

Abu Dhabi's enormous oil wealth has meant that it has been able to financially support the other Emirates, on both a collective and bilateral basis since before the formation of the UAE. Sheikh Zayed, as Ruler of Abu Dhabi, generously contributed to Trucial States Development Fund and became the fund's principal donor. After 1971, Abu Dhabi funded much of the Federal budget as well as providing support for less well-off Emirates bilaterally. This financial support has given Abu Dhabi significant influence in most of the other states. The notable exception to this has been Dubai which while lacking huge oil resources has for decades had a strong economy based on entrepôt trade, commerce and more recently property, financial services and tourism.

Demographically, oil has driven a massive change in the size and makeup of the Emirates' population. Exploiting oil reserves requires specialists, skilled trades people, literate workers and manual labourers. Given both the small Emirati population and their understandable lack of specialist skills during the early years of oil development, large numbers of foreign workers were required. In Abu Dhabi, the oil income funded a massive economic development program which saw the building of roads, electricity, water, hospitals and schools. Again, expatriates provided the vast bulk of the labour and skills for this development. Seeing the business opportunities arising from the expanding Abu Dhabi economy as well as in Dubai and Sharjah, expatriates also flowed into the country to establish businesses.

The growth in the population can be seen in the following census figures: in 1968, the population was 180,000. By 1971, it had grown to 287,000, in 1975 it was 557,000, by 1980 it had nearly doubled again to 1,042,000. By 1980, Emiratis made up just 27 percent of the population. The majority of expatriates in the Emirates have always been low skilled labourers and domestic workers from south Asian nations, notably Pakistan and India.

The large number of expatriates compared to nationals has long been a matter of concern for the Rulers and other nationals because it raises significant economic, social policy and security challenges. While foreigners are essential for labour and skills, their very significant presence has long been linked to social ills such as rising crime rates, unemployment of locals, drugs, prostitution, the spread of diseases, and the loss of traditional identity. From their beginnings, the Emirates' security services have been preparing for internal security operations linked to expatriates, such as protests, strikes and riots.

HISTORIC IMPORTANCE OF THE BRITISH

A notable feature of the early years of the Emirati security forces has been the strong British influence, which arose due to Britain's historic influence throughout the Gulf. British presence dates from the 1600s when the English East India Company (the Company) competed with the Portuguese and the Dutch for trade routes and rights in the region. By the early 1800s, the Company dominated trade in the Gulf as well as in India and Oman. With the help of the British military, the Company defeated the local maritime power of the lower Gulf, the Al Qawasem federation, and forced its leaders to sign a peace treaty, known as the General Maritime Treaty of 1820. This treaty required the Al Qawasem leaders to pledge not to attack other ships and to recognise Britain's right to enforce discipline and peace at sea. The British used this victory to encourage the other sheikhs ruling the littoral zones of the Lower Gulf (Dubai, Abu Dhabi and Bahrain) to sign similar treaties. This strategy resulted in Britain effectively becoming the dominant naval power in the Gulf. Further treaties were signed with the Rulers of the Lower Gulf including in 1853, the Perpetual Maritime Truce which made the truce enduring. It was from this agreement that the area became known as the Trucial States.

Britain's policy towards the Gulf in the mid-1800s focused on the waterway itself. Britain's priority was to ensure that its shipping and trading interests operated unhindered. Towards the late 1800s, an additional strategic priority for Britain was added – preventing the encroachment of other great powers into the region. Britain was concerned that if the influence of Russia, France or Germany spread to the Gulf, the eastern flank of the jewel in its colonial empire – British India – would be threatened.

To ensure that Britain maintained its exclusive regional dominance, in the late 1880s, Britain 'invited' the Lower Gulf Rulers to sign a new treaty, known as the Exclusive Agreement. It required that a Ruler would not enter into relationships with any power other than Britain, nor allow representatives of any foreign government to reside in his territory without British approval. It also prohibited the Rulers from disposing of any territory, including granting concessions, except to Britain. This arrangement would lead to Britain having an effective oil monopoly in the Trucial States in the following century. In return for signing the Exclusive Agreement, the land of a Ruler formally became a Protected State of Britain. This meant that Britain would be responsible for its defence and foreign relations. The Ruler would, however, retain sovereignty over his internal affairs apart from those deemed to have an impact on British external interests. All the Rulers of the Trucial States signed Exclusive Agreements between 1888 and 1892.

From the 1920s, Great Britain became more involved in the internal affairs of the Trucial States. Initially, this was driven by British desire to obtain both military and civil air facilities in the region so as to connect Britain with its eastern overseas territories–India, the Far East and Australia. The most important of these was the agreement between the Ruler of Sharjah and Britain to allow Imperial Airways to establish landing facilities near Sharjah township in 1932. The second driver was the prospect of finding oil and ensuring it was exploited by British companies. The first surface geological surveys by oil companies began in the 1930s, leading to the signing in 1939 of an oil concession agreement with the Ruler of Abu Dhabi. Oil exploration did not commence until after the Second World War, and when it did, it was impeded by insecurity. Banditry, tribal raids and even inter-emirate conflict (e.g. the 1945-1948 Abu Dhabi-Dubai War) were not uncommon, and the Rulers with their few armed retainers had little influence on security in the hinterlands. Another source of insecurity was distrust and animosity between the Rulers. Finally, tribal disputes were common over ownership of water wells, grazing land and even individual date palms.

To improve security and stability, in the late 1940s the British decided that a military should be permanently based in the Trucial States and tasked with building law, order and security. In 1951, the Trucial Oman Levies was formed. It was a British-led and officered, but locally-raised Arab force. Britain also supported the development of local security forces, which started with the formation of the Dubai Police and Abu Dhabi Police in the 1950s. Britain would continue this support when, during the 1960s, a number of Rulers established their own militaries and police forces. In most of these forces, British serving and contract officers filled the post of executive commanderss and in the larger ones, they made up a large percentage of their officer corps.

British support was provided in the form of (1) advice on the establishment of a force, (2) seconded officers and the recruitment of contract officers to serve as the force's commander, senior officers and specialists, (3) training teams and (4) allowing recruits to be trained at British military and police establishments, and (5) weapons and equipment.

In 1968, Britain announced it was going to withdraw its military forces from the region by 1971, and the Trucial States would no longer be protected by British forces. In December 1971, the Trucial States became a federation and became the UAE. Despite Britain's military withdrawal, it continued to provide significant numbers of seconded officers with many more British serving as contract officers.

During the 1970s, as more Emiratis and other expatriates were engaged by the Rulers, the British moved from executive positions to training and advising. By the end of the decade, there were only a few Britons left however, their legacy continued for decades afterwards as seen in the rank structure, uniforms, doctrine and structure of the UAE security forces.

2
TRUCIAL OMAN LEVIES/ TRUCIAL OMAN SCOUTS

The first modern military force to be raised in the Emirates was the British-controlled Trucial Oman Levies (TOL). Formed in 1951, the TOL's name was changed to Trucial Oman Scouts (TOS) in 1956 which continued to operate until 1971, before being handed over to the UAE and renamed the Union Defence Force.

Over its 20 years of existence, the TOL/TOS played a crucial role in the Emirates' security and military development. Its key achievements were to end the smuggling of slaves from Buraimi to Saudi Arabia, deterring Saudi Arabia from annexing parts of Abu Dhabi, assisting in counter-insurgency operations associated with Oman, and both preventing and calming tribal disputes. It was also instrumental in establishing most of the Emirati militaries and police forces. This was done through loaning its personnel to lead, manage and train these new forces, and making available its recruit training program for personnel from these new military forces. TOL/TOS members frequently formed the initial nucleus of the new forces, as the TOL/TOS allowed members of an Emirate to transfer to that Emirate's force even before their TOL/TOS service period ended. The TOL/TOS was a land force although it did occasionally use motorised *dhows* for coastal patrols and transport. It had no aircraft

Trucial Oman Scouts Mounted Troop. (Courtesy: William Naesmyth)

TOL overall and 1937-pattern belt, 1952. c. 1952. (Courtesy: Alistair MacDonald)

The headdress and collar badges of the TOL. The headdress badge of the TOL was a single dagger (*khunjar*). From 1953, British officers wore the silver crossed daggers shown top left. The single dagger is the headdress badge that was worn by Other Ranks. The smaller badges in the centre and bottom are collar badges. (Courtesy: Eddie Parks)

The TOL brass shoulder titles which were introduced for all TOL personnel in 1953. (Courtesy: Cliff Lord)

itself and relied on Britain's Royal Air Force (RAF) based at Sharjah and Bahrain for air support.

The decision to form the TOL was made by Britain's Foreign Office in 1948. The previous year, British administration in India had ended with India and Pakistan gaining independence. Before that time, British interests in the Gulf region had been administered not from London but via the head of the British administration in India, the Viceroy of India. Shifting responsibility for the Trucial States from India to London elevated interest in the region due to the potential for finding oil in the region. Of immediate concern to the British was the possible annexation of much of the potentially oil-rich Abu Dhabi Emirate by Saudi Arabia. In 1949, it had claimed some four fifths of the Emirate, including most of its coast to Mirfa, the western desert including Liwa, and the region around Al Ain. Having a permanent on-the-ground British military presence was seen as essential to addressing these strategic concerns.

On 11 May 1951, Britain issued a regulation establishing the TOL. At this time, the force was paid for, administered and directly controlled by the British Foreign Office rather than the War Office. This was because the force was seen as advancing British foreign interests, rather than military ones. Based at Sharjah, the force was under the direction of the British Political Residency in Bahrain, with responsibility delegated to a local Political Agent or Officer. As of 1951, the TOL was tasked with protecting the Political Residency's personnel, stopping the trade in slaves, and providing security in areas outside the direct control of a Ruling Sheikh.

To form the TOL, Jordan's Arab Legion was tasked with providing a team that could lead, recruit and train the new force. In 1951, a 35-man team arrived in Sharjah, headed by a British contract officer serving with the Arab Legion. This officer, Major J.M. (Michael) Hankin-Turvin, became the TOL's first commander.

The TOL was structured, trained and equipped as a *gendarmerie* (i.e. soldiers trained for police duties) rather than as an infantry force. To assist it in its policing duties, it was also given the power of arrest. At that time, the hinterland of the Emirates was described by one contemporary author as "little more than a battlefield for warring tribes, a haven for brigands and a profitable hunting ground for slave traders" as the Rulers' authority was limited to their coastal capitals. However, within just a year of the TOL's formation, there had been a marked improvement in the region's security. This was a considerable achievement given that the TOL numbered only around 60 by the end of 1951. The Political Resident at that time noted that he "was able to report no cases of abduction into slavery had occurred during the year and that the decrease in highway robbery was marked."

The original plan for the TOL was for Trucial States local citizens to be recruited, with a force of around 100 being built up over 18 months. However, this was a challenging goal as locals were suspicious of the force's role and therefore reluctant to join it. In addition, the poor health of the population meant that few of the volunteers were suitable for service. Consequently, Omanis (including Baluchis, Pakistanis and Dhofaris) and other nationalities were engaged initially, and while their numbers would reduce over the following two decades, the force still had many non-Emiratis serving in it up until 1971.

By mid-1952, the force's strength had reached 100. The force's concept of operations was to continually patrol the hinterland in order to deter crime, pursue criminals, and gather intelligence for both the British and the Rulers. They would intervene in local disputes over ownership of water, date palms and other resources in order to prevent them from escalating. If they could not settle disputes through arbitration, they would escalate the issue to be settled by the local Sheikh, Ruler or the British political representative. Where tensions remained high after a dispute or a threat was identified,

The belt buckle of the TOS. The Arabic script under the crossed *khunjars* reads 'Force of the Oman Coast', rather than a direct translation of the English name. (Courtesy: Cliff Lord)

The initial brass shoulder title of the TOS. (Courtesy: Cliff Lord)

Badges and buttons of the TOS. With the re-naming of the TOL to TOS, the officers' headdress badge was altered to include cannons and a scroll. The Arabic script under the crossed daggers reads 'Force of the Oman Coast'. The silver buttons were only worn by TOS officers. ORs and NCOs of the TOS continued to wear the single dagger badge. (Courtesy: Eddie Parks)

Major J. M. Hankin-Turvin, founding commander of the TOL. He was a contract officer detached from the Jordan Arab Legion who served in the TOL from 1951 to 1953. He is wearing the headdress badge of the Arab Legion. The initial uniform of the TOL was that of the Arab Legion. It consisted of a long khaki cloak (*thaub*) worn over white trousers. A red *shemagh* with black *agal* was worn on the head but without a badge. Personnel also wore a crossed bandolier and belt. (Courtesy: UAE National Archives)

the force would establish a post in that location, manned by a small detachment. When security was re-established, the post would be removed.

In August 1952, an armed force from Saudi Arabia occupied the Omani village in the Buraimi Oases. Britain, which had treaty arrangements for the protection of both the Trucial States and Oman, chose not to respond militarily to the Saudi occupation, and convinced both the Ruler of Abu Dhabi and the Sultan of Oman likewise. Instead, Britain sought to resolve the situation peacefully. In November 1952, a standstill agreement was reached with Saudi Arabia, which allowed Saudi and British forces to remain in their present positions in the Oases while negotiations for a peaceful settlement were undertaken. Both sides agreed not to reinforce their force nor to seek to subvert local tribes via bribery or coercion.

As it was recognised that the existing TOL was not capable of assaulting occupied positions or of effectively guarding the Trucial States' borders against further Saudi encroachments, in early 1953 Britain decided to increase the TOL to 500. Given that an increase of this size would take a while to effect, in the meantime the British brought in reinforcements for the TOL. In January 1953, a detachment of RAF armoured cars arrived, and, starting in February 1953, the first of over 300 of the RAF-controlled Aden Protectorate Levies arrived. To build up TOL numbers, several hundred discharged Adeni soldiers were recruited on two-year contracts. By August 1953, the requisite strength of the TOL was reached which allowed the Aden Protectorate Levies to return to Aden.

Many of the former recruited Adeni soldiers turned out to be unreliable and they frequently engaged in criminal behaviour. Following several incidents, which culminated in a mutiny by one of the Adeni-manned TOS Squadrons and the murder of two British officers and an NCO by Adeni soldiers in Al Ain/Buraimi area in November 1953, nearly all of the 90-man Adenese Squadron were dismissed. They were replaced over the following few months with local citizens and non-locals recruited from the region.

While initially the War Office had minimal involvement with the TOL, the Saudi activity in Buraimi led to a request for greater British Army engagement. In early 1952, the first British Army officer arrived to serve in the TOL. He was followed by several others, and all accelerated the force's professionalism through their training and leadership. With the return to Jordan of Major Hankin-

A TOL officer wearing the TOL badge which at that stage lacked the scroll under the crossed daggers. (Courtesy: Tom Wylie Belfast Museum)

TOS demonstrating the British 2-inch mortar. (Courtesy: Sharjah Police)

Turvin in August 1953, the first serving British Army officer (Lieutenant Colonel W.J. Martin) became the commander of the TOL. In 1954, the force formally became a shared responsibility with the War Office.

From this point onwards, British Army officers would command and fill most officer posts in TOL/TOS units. Arab officers invariably filled only junior posts. British Army NCOs also served in the force, mostly in training and specialist roles. English was the language of the force's headquarters, as well as signals and technical training. The language used in the force's combat units was Arabic. This meant that British officers in the force squadrons needed to speak Arabic, and they would generally attend an Arabic language course before joining the force.

By the end of 1954, the TOL was structured into an HQ squadron at Sharjah and three 100-man Rifle Squadrons. The force's total strength was just over 500 men, 14 of whom were British. The OCs and 2ICs of the Rifle Squadrons were British officers, as were all of the HQ staff. One Rifle Squadron was based in the Al Ain region watching the Buraimi Oasis, another was at Sharjah to provide security for the region and the TOL HQ, and the third was based at Tarif where continuation training was done. The selection of a camp at Tarif on the western coast of Abu Dhabi was to stop Saudi subversive activities in the region, including around Liwa, as well as to provide protection for local oil exploration activities. Each squadron was tactically mounted in its own transport (Land Rovers and Bedford trucks), allowing it to move at short notice and operate independently.

In July 1954, Saudi Arabia and Britain signed the Jeddah Agreement which referred the Buraimi issue to an impartial international tribunal headed by a Belgian judge of the International Court. Despite this development, Saudi Arabia continued to subvert

British units involved in countering the Saudi occupation of parts of Buraimi in 1953. Left to right: an Aden Protectorate Levy officer; Captain Peter MacDonald TOL; Sheikh Zayed bin Sultan Al Nahyan, Governor of Al Ain and future Ruler of Abu Dhabi and President of the UAE; and Flight Lieutenant Bill Turner RAF Regiment. By 1952, TOS personnel wore the British Army tropical uniform which consisted of a khaki drill shirt and trousers, or olive drab denim trousers and blouse for fatigues. Footwear was brown leather sandals known as 'Sandals, Muscat Levies', or black canvas PT shoes. Personnel were also issued with a khaki wool pullover, British Army greatcoat for winter wear, and 1937 pattern webbing belt and accoutrements. (Courtesy: Alistair MacDonald)

the loyalty of Omani and Abu Dhabi tribes in the region through bribery and intimidation. By 1955, Saudi Arabia's behaviour had become so egregious that Britain abandoned the tribunal's dispute settlement process and ordered a military operation to forcefully expel the Saudis from Buraimi. On 26 October 1955, two TOL squadrons assaulted the positions of the Saudi forces and their allied tribesmen. The action was supported to a limited degree by Abu Dhabi tribesmen, Omani forces and regular British forces. The operation was successful, although two TOL soldiers were killed and three wounded. Up to 11 dissident tribesmen were also killed but no Saudis. All the Saudis were deported and a number of their allied tribesmen went into exile.

Despite the success of the operation, it revealed significant weaknesses in the TOL, including its inability to effectively operate as an infantry force due to a lack of manpower, training and heavy infantry weapons. Consequently, the force was up-armed, expanded and formally given the mission of defending the Trucial States borders. The expansion plan called for a fifth rifle squadron to be added, for each rifle squadron to be expanded from 94 to 150 men, and for the formation of both a training wing and a mortar platoon.

To build this new force, the TOL required a substantial increase in British personnel. To encourage more British serving personnel to volunteer, the force's name was changed in 1956, substituting the word 'scout' for 'levies'. This was to eliminate the impression that the force was conscripted, and it made the force sound more exotic and alluring. By 1960-1961, their number had increased from a handful to around 40 British officers and 100 NCOs. The TOS's disposition in the late 1950s also changed, with squadrons redeployed to protect oil exploration in the west of Abu Dhabi Emirate as well as to the Northern Emirates to enhance internal security.

The TOS's conventional infantry capabilities grew in the late 1950s as it became involved in operations in neighbouring Oman. In the mid-1950s, a separatist movement developed in Oman's interior. Headed by the Imam of the Islamic Ibadhi sect, it sought to establish an independent interior state. After the separatists defeated the Sultan of Oman's forces in 1957, the TOS forces were tasked with supporting British and Omani forces that were fighting to reassert the Sultan's authority. The separatists were finally defeated in 1959, following which all TOS forces were withdrawn from Oman. This was the first and last time the TOS was deployed outside of the Emirates, however it would be involved in efforts within the Emirates to disrupt the flow of men and materiel to support the Dhofar Rebellion in southern Oman (1962 to 1976).

The TOS grew considerably in size over the late 1950s. In 1956, the force's strength was 680 men, and in May 1960 was nearly 1,300. Local citizens from the Trucial States made up the minority of the force at this time, accounting for 450 of the 1,150 non-British enlisted personnel. By the end of the 1950s, the TOS was structured into five 120-man Rifle Squadrons, named as A, B, C, D and X Squadrons, and a Support Group, under a single force HQ. It also had a substantial HQ squadron which included a large workshop, a Transport troop, signal centre, Signal Squadron, a small hospital, a Pipe Band, and a Training Squadron.

In August 1960, concerns that the TOS might again need to be involved in combat operations resulted in a restructure. The force was split into two components – the Desert Regiment with its own HQ, which focused on conventional infantry combat, and the Trucial States Regiment with its HQ in Sharjah, which focused on

Table 2: Trucial Oman Levies/Trucial Oman Scouts	
Political head	**Executive commander**
Political Resident Persian Gulf (Bahrain)	**Commander TOL/TOS**
1946-1953: W.R. (William) Rupert Hay	1951-1953: Major J.M. (Michael) Hankin-Turvin
1953-1958: B.A.B. (Bernard) Burrows	1953-1954: Lieutenant Colonel W.J. Martin
1958-1961: G.H. (George) Middleton	1954-1957: Colonel E.F. Johnston
1961-1966: W.H.T. (William) Luce	1957-1961: Colonel S.L.A. (Stewart) Carter
1966-1970: R.S. (Robert) Crawford	1961-1964: Colonel H.J. (Bart) Bartholomew
1970-1971: G. (Geoffrey) Arthur	1964-1967: Colonel F.M. (Freddie) de Butts
Delegated to:	1967-1970: Colonel K.P.G. (Pat) Ive
1948-1951: P. D. Stobart, Political Officer, Sharjah	1970-1971: Colonel H.E.R. (Roy) Watson
1951-1952: A. John Wilton, Political Officer, Sharjah	
1952-1955: M.S. (Michael) Weir, Political Officer, Sharjah/Dubai	
1954-1955: C.M. (Christopher) Pirie-Gordon, Political Officer, Dubai	
1955-1958: John Peter Tripp, Political Officer, Dubai	
1958-1961: Donald F. Hawley, Political Officer, Dubai	
1961-1964: Alfred James M. Craig, Political Agent, Dubai	
1964-1966: H. Glencairn Balfour-Paul, Political Agent, Dubai	
1966-1968: David A. Roberts, Political Agent, Dubai	
1969-1971: Julian L. Bullard, Political Agent, Dubai	
1971: Julian Fortay Walker, Political Agent, Dubai	
1956–1958: Martin Buckmaster, Political Officer, Abu Dhabi	
1958–1959: Edric R. Worsnop, Political Officer, Abu Dhabi	
1959-1961: Edward F. Henderson, Political Officer, Abu Dhabi	
1961-1965: Colonel Sir Hugh Boustead, Political Agent, Abu Dhabi	
1965–1968: Sir Archie T. Lamb, Political Agent, Abu Dhabi	
1968–1971: C.J. (James) Treadwell, Political Agent, Abu Dhabi	

TOS mortar detachment under training using the British 3-inch mortar Mk 5 barrel, No 6 baseplate, Mk 5 bipod. (Courtesy: Sharjah Police)

TOS squadron officer, Captain D. Neild, working in his palm fond (*arish*) office in Sharjah, 1959. He was only 20 years old when he joined the TOS, making him the youngest British officer ever to serve in the TOS. He would later become the founding commander for both the Ras Al Khaimah Mobile Force and Sharjah National Guard. (Courtesy: David Neild)

the traditional TOS internal security mission. In addition, the HQ in Sharjah was expanded and staffed to run a Brigade should there be an emergency. By mid-1961, it was decided that this two-force structure was not appropriate. This was because the capabilities of Omani forces had improved to the point where it had become unlikely that the TOS would again be involved in operations outside the Trucial States. In addition, the two HQ command structure had been found to be cumbersome. In September 1961, the Desert Regiment was disbanded, with the force returning to its earlier structure – five Rifle Squadrons under a single HQ supported by both HQ Squadron and Training Squadron.

Also, in 1961, Major Stevenson raised a group of pipers and drummers, which were taken to Aden for music instruction.

Two TOS workshop fitters at Hijar, below Jebel Akhdar, in the 1960s. They are wearing red and white chequered *shemaghs* with the black *agal*, which was introduced in 1957, 1937 pattern web belts, and wear their jumpers tucked into their trousers. (Courtesy: Tony Ford)

Warrant Officer Tim Ash of the Signal Squadron alongside recruit signaller Ahmed, from the TOS Boys' School, c. 1966. The Warrant Officer is wearing a loose-fitting blue-grey *mazri* cotton shirt which was introduced in 1958. It was worn open at the neck with collar badges, and outside the trousers in warmer months. It had a slit on either side at waist level, while the bottom of the shirt was at the top of the thigh. The sleeves were often rolled up. The trousers were khaki drill. Shorts were not worn except for boys attending the Boys' School. The photo shows the Warrant Officer wearing Clarks Desert Boots and the boy wearing sandals, which had a full heel with a U-shaped steel plate. The leather came up over the toes and had a strap across the foot with a brass buckle to fasten them. (Courtesy: Tim Ash)

Major Jacques took over this successful band two years later. The TOS Pipes and Drums were a feature at important parades and ceremonial occasions.

The operational concept for the TOS for the 1960s onwards with respect to the threat from Saudi Arabia was that the TOS would just slow a Saudi advance, rather than resist a committed attack. This would give time for British regular forces to assemble and counter-attack.

A system of regular rotation for the Rifle Squadrons had by then been introduced. Known as the 'Squadron Roundabout', this involved the squadrons moving roughly every four to six months through each outstation in turn, plus Sharjah where one squadron was co-located with the TOS HQ. In 1962, the outstations were at Masafi in the Hajar Mountains, Manama, Jahili Fort at Al Ain, and Mirfa on Abu Dhabi's western coast close to the key oilfield area of Tarif. The rotation system was designed both to prevent relationships developing between the troops and the local citizens, which was seen as potentially inhibiting the force's impartiality, and to provide respite from the more uncomfortable camps. Outstations would sometimes maintain subordinate posts where a detachment from a squadron would be deployed. Both outstations and posts moved locations from time to time to reflect changing security needs, such as new flashpoints of tribal disputes, countering Saudi subversion efforts, and locations where oil drilling parties operated and needed security.

The internal security functions of the TOS in the early 1960s

continued as before – intervening in and de-escalating tribal disputes, deterring crime and apprehending criminals in the hinterland (including gun-smuggling, principally from Saudi Arabia, Egypt and other countries which were supporting separatist and revolutionary groups in Oman), and protecting the movement of the Political Residency staff and British oil operations. The TOS was also involved in maintaining public order in settlements. For example, in April 1963, a mob of dissatisfied labourers and unemployed trouble makers attempted to invade the airfield at Sharjah but were deterred by the TOS's presence. The TOS also settled labour protests due to their presence in 1963 on Abu Dhabi's key oil exporting facility at Das Island.

Infrequently, the force was called upon to help to re-establish or reinforce the authority of a Ruler. One of the first of these occasions was in July 1952 when the TOL assisted the Ruler of Ras Al Khaimah to retake a fort occupied by a rebel sheikh in the Rams area. The force could also occasionally intervene in disputes within a Ruling Family. For example, in 1955, the force assisted the Ruler of Dubai to prevent his overthrow by a relative.

The force was involved in two operations to replace Rulers. These were only undertaken after the Residency had obtained the consent of the relevant Ruling Family. The first such operation was in 1965 when the TOS supported the deposition of the Ruler of Sharjah, Sheikh Saqr bin Sultan Al Qasimi. Sheikh Saqr was an outspoken nationalist and supporter of pan-Arabism, who was seen by the British as seeking to undermine their position, and he lacked support from his Ruling Family. The second was in 1966 when the TOS facilitated the replacement of the Ruler of Abu Dhabi, Sheikh Shakhbut bin Sultan Al Nahyan, due to concerns that he was impeding state development.

The TOS in the early 1960s continued to grow and by February 1964 had an establishment strength of 1,235 personnel. In the late 1960s efforts were made to improve both the uniform and equipment of the TOS. This was necessary because Major 'Tug' Wilson, Commander of the Abu Dhabi Defence Force, had designed very smart uniforms for his force and they were proving popular with the Arab Officers and men. Consequently, the then TOS Commanding Officer, Colonel Ive, introduced a new jacket in grey material for all officers, with silver buttons, bearing crossed *khunjahs*.

British Army ranks were used by all members of the TOL/TOS. Officers' rank badges wore those used by the British Army with the exception of the Commander's Arab Commissioned officers who wore silver stars instead of pips. Arab Second Lieutenants with a Queen's Commission had a red star rank badge on the shoulder. Arab Second Lieutenants with a Commander's Commission had a white star. The red star indicated that the officer should be treated the same as a British officer and enjoyed the same privileges. The white star showed that the officer was to be treated as an officer by the Arab troops but not by the British as he did not have a Queen's Commission and had not attended a military academy. NCO ranks wore standard chevrons in white tape worn on the right arm, TOS Warrant Officers wore standard British Army brass rank badges on a wrist strap of blue-grey material.

In 1966, the British Government announced it was going to withdraw its forces from Aden following years of anti-British, pan-Arabic and revolutionary political agitation and revolt. As the British feared their departure would embolden groups hostile to its presence in the Gulf, the British military presence in the Trucial States expanded considerably. This included basing some 2,400 British personnel in Sharjah. To make space for these troops, the TOS elements in Sharjah were moved to a newly constructed camp

Warrant Officer Class II (*Wakeel*) Ahmed Musaád, the Arab Squadron Sergeant Major of the Signal Squadron, c. 1967. (Courtesy: Tim Ash)

TOS Corporal Bob Lowe, Signal Squadron (centre), on camel familiarisation activity on the track between Sharjah and the TOS's Manama camp, 1961. (Courtesy: Bob Lowe)

A TOS Staff Sergeant and Captain Keith Stewart talking to *bedu* in the late 1950s. Although camel-based patrols were used for difficult terrain, motorised ones were far more common. (Courtesy: Keith Stewart)

A group of British instructors attending a passing out parade at the TOS Training Squadron camp, Manama, in 1967. Left to right: Pipe Major McPhee, Sergeant Joe Hubble, Warrant Officer Class II CSM Mickey Munn, and RSM Nichol. With the exception of the RSM, they are wearing red stable belts and ceremonial sashes. The belts were not worn at all times as they created restriction around the waistline in the heat. (Courtesy: Brian "Tug" Wilson)

to provide security and stability for the Emirates as they transitioned from protected states to a fully sovereign nation. Britain advanced the idea that the TOS could become the nucleus of a collective force for a federation of the Lower Gulf states. It offered to transfer the force to the new federal state, to continue to allow British personnel to serve in it, and to sell or gift its weapons, equipment and facilities to the new state.

In the final years of its treaty responsibilities, Britain worked to ensure the TOS remained a viable force. In 1969, it re-equipped the force with modern British infantry weapons including SLRs. In July 1971, the Rulers of the Trucial States (except for Ras Al Khaimah) all agreed to form a federated state which came into existence on 2 December 1971. They agreed to assume responsibility for the TOS.

Despite Britain's treaty responsibilities ending on 1 December 1971, the TOS continued to exist as a British-led force until it was disbanded at midnight on 21 December 1971. At this point it had

at Murqaab, a few miles north-west of Sharjah in September 1967.

In January 1968, Britain announced it would withdraw its forces from the Gulf by the end of 1971, which meant it would end its control of the TOS. However, Britain wanted the TOS to continue

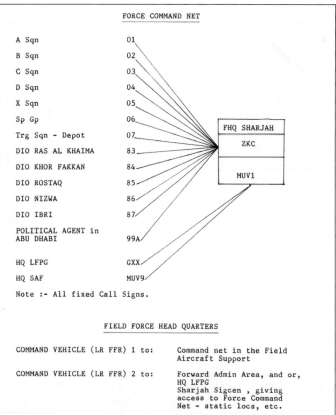

```
                    FORCE COMMAND NET

    A Sqn                   01
    B Sqn                   02
    C Sqn                   03
    D Sqn                   04
    X Sqn                   05
    Sp Gp                   06            ┌─────────────┐
    Trg Sqn - Depot         07            │ FHQ SHARJAH │
    DIO RAS AL KHAIMA       83            │    ZKC      │
    DIO KHOR FAKKAN         84            │             │
    DIO ROSTAQ              85            │    MUV1      │
    DIO NIZWA               86            └─────────────┘
    DIO IBRI                87
    POLITICAL AGENT in
    ABU DHABI               99A

    HQ LFPG                 GXX
    HQ SAF                  MUV9

    Note :- All fixed Call Signs.


              FIELD FORCE HEAD QUARTERS

    COMMAND VEHICLE (LR FFR) 1 to:    Command net in the Field
                                      Aircraft Support

    COMMAND VEHICLE (LR FFR) 2 to:    Forward Admin Area, and or,
                                      HQ LFPG
                                      Sharjah Sigcen , giving
                                      access to Force Command
                                      Net - static locs, etc.
```

The TOS's Force Command Net as of the late 1960s. It shows the call signs of the force's various elements and commands. As well as the rifle squadrons (A to X Squadron), the net included the TOS's heavy infantry weapons Support Group and the Training Squadron at Manama. Each of the Desert Intelligence Officers (DIOs) had their own radios. The net not only connected DIOs in the Emirates (i.e. in Ras Al Khaimah and Khor Fakkan) but also in Oman (i.e Rostaq, Nizwa and Ibri). The TOS net had direct radio contact with the local British political representative in Abu Dhabi (but not in Dubai as this was probably done via landlines), as well as the TOS's superior headquarters, Land Forces Persian Gulf (LFPG) in Bahrain, and HQ Sultan's Armed Forces (SAF). Crypto security was provided by portable off line cipher eqipment. (Courtesy: Tim Ash)

35 British officers, 33 Arab officers and a total strength of around 1,500 personnel. All locally engaged personnel were discharged, and along with its serving British officers and NCOs, all were invited to join a new force, the Union Defence Force (UDF), under the control of the UAE Government. Virtually all did, including all the British officers who then became seconded officers. This resulted in the UDF having the same personnel as the TOS, continuing the traditional of the British holding all the senior posts, including Commander and Deputy Commander, and all OC Squadrons and senior Staff Officers' posts.

TRUCIAL OMAN SCOUTS POLICE WING

At the beginning of the 1960s, only Abu Dhabi and Dubai had police forces. In the other five Emirates, security in their capital towns was provided by Ruler's armed retainers and guards. The limited finances of these Rulers meant that they could not afford to establish police forces nor were such forces then justified given their Emirates' low population and crime rate.

Around this time, the British started questioning if this would continue to be the most appropriate policing arrangements for these Emirates. Britain's Political Agent in Dubai, Donald Hawley, arranged for a colonial police expert, Robert Waggitt, to conduct a review of policing in the five Emirates in 1961. He recommended that the TOS form a police troop (later known as the TOS Police Wing) which would be responsible for these Emirates. Like the rest of the TOS, the Police Wing was restricted to operating in areas outside the Rulers' capital towns and could only enter them with express approval. However, it was hoped that as the Rulers' confidence grew in the Wing's capabilities, it would be invited to operate in their towns.

The plan for the Wing was for it to have an establishment strength of 35, function as a small mobile police unit, and headed by a professional police officer with experience in the region. The formation of the Police Wing started in the first half of 1963 with the arrival of its commander, the British police officer, Mr Jack Briggs who was given the rank of a Major. He had served in the Palestine Police Force and his immediate previous post was as Deputy Commander of Qatar Police Force. His first task was to recruit members for his Wing, develop a police training program, and to build support among the Rulers to allow the police to operate in their capital towns.

The missions of the Police Wing were to suppress crime, undertake criminal investigations, execute warrants, operate a prison, suppress illegal migration and stop the traffic in slaves, narcotics and illegal arms, ammunition and explosives. The Wing was based in Sharjah within the TOS Headquarters Squadron.

Central to the success of the Police Wing was that the Rulers would invite the Wing to function in their capital towns. This was because this was the most effective way to prevent crime rather than patrolling the hinterland. Despite Major Briggs and others' efforts to convince the Rulers to allow this, they did not agree. This fatally undermined the utility of the Police Wing and consequently, by early 1965, it was decided to disband the troop. Its members were dispersed to the rest of the TOS, resulting in Major Briggs not having a function. When the Police Commandant of Dubai was sacked by its Ruler in May 1965, the Ruler offered him this post, which he accepted and resigned from the TOS.

TOS *DHOW* PATROL

The Trucial Oman Scouts did not have a maritime force, however over its existence it used *dhows* for various purposes. Originally they were used just to transport men and goods for resupplying bases but in the early 1960s, it had on permanent lease a diesel-powered fast *dhow* – the *Al Qaid*. This could undertake three-day patrols so as to counter smuggling, gun-running and illegal immigration, and with its top speed of eight knots, could overhaul most vessels at the time. RAF Shackletons sometimes vectored the *Al Qaid* on to suspect craft, and the vessel carried a section of the TOS armed with rifles and a Bren gun. During winter, one of the main tasks was to deliver rations to the Mirfa Squadron when the *sabkha* areas were impassable. The boat had a radio and was on a radio schedule with Sharjah HQ. Some of the other tasks of the *dhow* patrol were to visit villages that could not be reached by road and check for smallpox, and to monitor the water wells' state.

MOUNTED TROOP

In 1958, a TOS officer went to Baghdad to purchase horses for the TOS. Fifteen horses were brought to Sharjah, initially for the officers' recreational purposes but around 1960 a ceremonial troop of cavalry was formed. The troop wore white ceremonial uniforms and carried lances, and escorted important visitors and were prominent during important parades. They became a feature of the TOS throughout the rest of its existence, although due to the high cost of their upkeep, in 1968 the number of horses had been reduced to eight.

Figure 3: Structure of the TOS, 1967

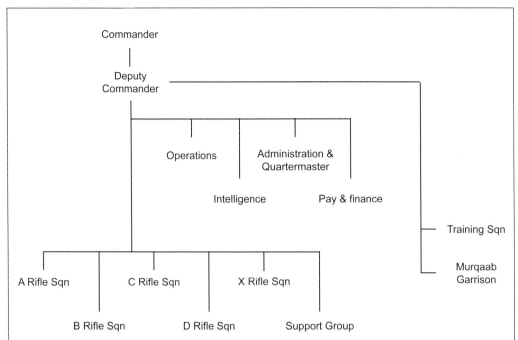

Trucial Oman Scouts LWB Land Rover FFR and used as a Radio Command Vehicle when Force HQ deployed in the field. A British C13 radio was used to communicate with TOS HQ in Sharjah and a C11 radio with HQ LFPG in Bahrain, c. 1965-1967. (Courtesy: Tim Ash)

3

ABU DHABI DEFENCE FORCE

The first Ruler-controlled military in the Emirates was established by the Abu Dhabi Ruler, Sheikh Shakhbut bin Sultan Al Nahyan, in 1965. The original concept was to have a small, land-based force which had two key roles – being a bodyguard for the Sheikh, and guarding the Al Maqta causeway which was the only crossing point from the mainland to Abu Dhabi Island, where the Ruler's fort and Abu Dhabi town were located. The force was to be made up of locally-raised Arab troops led by two British officers. Their role was to "organise, train and command the force" as well as to advise his son, Sheikh Sultan, who was to be the force's Commander-in-Chief. Given the Sheikh's lack of professional military expertise, he accepted a plan for the force developed by Major General E.S. Lindsay, MoD (UK), submitted in October 1964.

THE FORMATION

While the British preferred that the Ruler relied on the TOS rather than forming his own personal military, by 1964 they had somewhat reluctantly come to support the concept of an Abu Dhabi army. One benefit was that the force would reduce British military expenditure as it would allow TOS squadrons on Abu Dhabi soil to be withdrawn. Secondly, the force was seen as enhancing British security objectives. Having a well-run and disciplined force, commanded by seconded British officers and owing allegiance only to the Ruler, and which would co-operate with the Trucial Oman

Scouts in the defence and internal security of Abu Dhabi" would help to counter the instability in eastern Arabia and the ongoing unresolved border dispute between Abu Dhabi and Saudi Arabia.

The plan for the force was refined, and by early 1965 its strength was planned as two British officers, one Arab Warrant Officer and 213 men. The two British officers arrived in the second half of 1965. They were TOS officers who had been temporarily attached to the Abu Dhabi force. Major (later Colonel) E.B. (Tug) Wilson and Captain (later Lieutenant Colonel) C.W. (Charles) Wontner filled the posts of Commander and Deputy Commander respectively.

During 1966, it was planned that the force would be structured into two rifle squadrons which were to be deployed at strategic locations to counter Saudi Arabia. These locations were Al Hamra on the coastal route between Qatar and Abu Dhabi, and at Al Ain. At that time, the TOS had outstations at Al Ain and at Tarif to the east of Al Hamra. By the end of 1965, it was decided that the ADDF motorised light infantry force, mounted in Land Rovers and Bedford trucks, was to be augmented by two Ferret scout car troops, and a troop of medium mortars. By June 1966, the force's strength reached 158, consisting of two British and four Arab officers, 13 NCOs, 59 trained soldiers, another 60 undertaking recruit training plus 20 civilians and enlisted followers.

Sheikh Shakbut's immediate expansion plans were to increase the number of British officers from 2 to 9 to support the expansion

of the force to 250. The short-term force structure plan was a Rifle Squadron to be permanently based at Al Hamra with a troop stationed at Liwa, and a camp in Al Ain with a troop patrolling in that area.

In August 1966, the Ruling Family, facilitated by the British, replaced the Ruler of Abu Dhabi with his brother, Sheikh Zayed. To ensure a peaceful transition, the TOS closed the Al Maqta causeway to prevent the arrival of any tribesmen loyal to Sheikh Shakhbut, and surrounded the Ruler's fort on Abu Dhabi Island. Sheikh Shakhbut initially refused to step aside and remained in his fort protected by his personal retainers. While the Abu Dhabi military was there to protect Sheikh Shakhbut, it remained in barracks. Recognising his lack of support, Sheikh Shakhbut surrendered and was escorted by the TOS to the Abu Dhabi airstrip and flown into exile by the Royal Air Force.

Upon his accession, Sheikh Zayed immediately sought to expand the force, now formally known as the Abu Dhabi Defence Force (ADDF). As of September 1966, plans were for the ADDF to expand to between 800 and 1,000 men over the following two to three years, but soon after, this number increased to 1,500 men. The operational concept of the force was that it would work in cooperation with friendly forces (i.e. the TOS and British regular forces) "in resisting any threat to the integrity of the State as well as performing its internal security role". Its force structure was to be one infantry

Sheikh Zayed bin Sultan Al Nahyan, Supreme Commander of the ADDF and Ruler of Abu Dhabi, shaking hands with Commander Giles St. George Poole, Commander ADDF Sea Wing. Behind Sheikh Zayed left to right are Dawood Siksik, a Secretary in the Ruler's Court, Sheikh Mubarak bin Mohammed Al Nahyan, Commandant of Abu Dhabi Police, and Abu Dhabi Police personnel, wearing black and white *shemaghs*. The three officers on the left hand side of the picture are, from left to right, Colonel E.B. Wilson, Commander ADDF, Lieutenant Colonel Peter MacDonald, ADDF Deputy Commander, and Squadron Leader Jim Timms, ADDF Air Wing. (Courtesy: UAE National Archive, c. 1968)

battalion, an armoured squadron and an artillery battery, in addition to logistics and support companies. It would be supported by an air wing of four light aircraft and a sea wing of five patrol launches. Such expansion required an increase in expertise, and large scale recruitment of both seconded and contracted British personnel started. The next officer to arrive was the first contracted officer, Major (later Colonel) Peter MacDonald, joining on 18 August 1966. Sheikh Zayed had asked for Major MacDonald personally as he had worked with him in 1953 when Major MacDonald was a Squadron Commander based in Al Ain during the start of the Buraimi crisis. A priority was establishing the Recruit Depot, and this had occurred by the end of 1966. Contracted British officers founded and commanded the Depot, with local and other Arab NCOs providing recruit instruction.

The scale of the 1966 expansion was of concern to the British as reflected in the comment by the British Resident that it would create "the fashion for private armies which was feared would inevitably spread up the coast." The British wanted Sheikh Zayed to agree to put the ADDF under political direction by the Political Resident, and operational control of the TOS Commander. He rejected this but did mollify Britain's concern by stating that he would be committed to the fullest cooperation with the TOS.

In January 1968, the British Government unexpectedly announced that it would withdraw its forces in the Gulf by 1971. This had two key implications from Abu Dhabi's perspective. Firstly, it was now unlikely that strong, friendly forces would come to the aid of Abu Dhabi in the event of external aggression. Secondly, the region would become more unpredictable due to the loss of Britain's stabilising influence. This perception resulted in major changes being made to both the role of and capability needed for the ADDF. In September 1968, the Force consisted of one Ferret scout car squadron, three rifle squadrons and a Royal Guard squadron, one troop of 81mm mortars, a combined HQ Squadron and Signal Troop, a combined Transport and Workshop squadron and a Training Depot. The Sea Wing had three 40ft patrol craft and the Air Wing the first two transport aircraft plus two tactical helicopters.

The force's roles were now defined as (1) guaranteeing the integrity of the State against external interference, and (2) maintaining peace and good order within the State, particularly the prevention of subversion and illegal immigration. The ADDF's size and structure changed, with the goal now being to establish – before Britain's 1971 departure – a roughly brigade-sized force (expected to be about 3-4,000 men) that was highly mobile and had close air support. It would also need an enhanced sea patrol capability for border security. The planned force structure consisted of (1) Land Forces made up of an Armoured Reconnaissance Regiment, a Support Regiment of 81mm mortars and/or 105mm pack howitzers, two Infantry Battalions, a Signal Squadron, HQ Squadron, a Royal Guard Squadron, a Transport Squadron, Field Ambulance, Ordnance Depot, Armoured/Infantry Workshop, and a Training Depot including an Arab Officers' Academy and Boys' Training School; (2) Sea Wing made up of six 40ft and three appreciably larger patrol craft; and (3) Air Wing made up of a transport and communications squadron consisting of Caribou, Islander and Jet Ranger flights.

While the Political Resident recognised that Abu Dhabi needed an effective defence force, he was concerned that "it must not expand too much or have weapons which would make it look provocative" to the neighbouring Rulers and states. In addition, there was concern that a strong Abu Dhabi force would undermine efforts to form a federation of Lower Gulf Emirates which had got

underway in early 1968, and in particular the British-preferred post-1971 solution of basing a military to protect this federation around the TOS. As well as trying to convince Sheikh Zayed to reduce the force's expansion, the Political Resident made efforts to impede the ADDF from obtaining sophisticated equipment.

The ADDF Air Wing was formed in May 1968 to provide both air transport for the ADDF and a ground attack capability to support ADDF land forces. The first aircraft came into service in late 1968 and by mid-1971 the Air Wing consisted of a force of ground attack aircraft, light helicopters and utility aircraft. Two Britten-Norman Islander aircraft were the first aircraft to arrive. Ideal for desert conditions, these short take-off and landing (STOL) light transport aircraft could carry up to 9 passengers and were based at the recently built runway at the Al Bateen Air Base and Airport. By the end of the same year, they were followed by two Augusta-Bell 206A Jet Rangers. These light helicopters could carry three passengers, and were used primarily for casualty evacuation, liaison and observation. Further orders included two Bell 205 helicopters (civilian versions of the UH-1 Iroquois single-engine military helicopter), and three DHC-4 Caribou tactical transport aircraft. Twelve Hawker Hunters Mk 9 (10 FGA 76 single seat and two T77 two-seat trainers) were ordered. These aircraft arrived from mid-1970 to mid-1971. With the engagement of experienced, mostly British-contracted, Hawker Hunter pilots, the ADDF Air Wing rapidly developed a very effective ground attack and an (albeit limited) air defence capability.

Two more Jet Rangers and two DHC-4 tactical transport aircraft arrived by 1971. As of the end of 1971, the Air Wing structure consisted of one Squadron of Hunters, and one Squadron of transport aircraft made up of three Flights – one each of Bell 205 helicopters, Caribou tactical transport aircraft and Islander light transport aircraft.

Abu Dhabi's naval force was the smallest of the three services. Established in April 1967, the role of the Sea Wing was to patrol the Emirate's territorial waters, and to be seen, thus acting to deter smugglers and illegal migrants, and to protect offshore oil infrastructure from possible attack. The force received its first patrol boats in 1968, and by 1970, its fleet consisted of six 40ft small coastal patrol boats and three 56ft patrol boats. The smaller vessels were armed with a 0.5" machine gun and two 0.303" Bren guns on the flying bridge, while the latter had two 20mm cannons and two 7.62mm machine guns. The Sea Wing's main base and headquarters was near the Al Nahyan Military Camp on Abu Dhabi Island.

FORCE RESTRUCTURES

Until 1969, the command structure of the ADDF consisted of the Commander ADDF reporting directly to the Ruler of Abu Dhabi. Supporting the Commander was the Deputy Commander, who was in turn supported by a small staff. This changed in February 1969 with the establishment of the Abu Dhabi Department of Defence and the post of Chairman of Defence. The Commander ADDF now reported to the Chairman, a position filled by Sheikh Khalifa bin Zayed Al Nahyan, the son of the Ruler of Abu Dhabi and Crown Prince from 1969, who reported to the Ruler as the force's Supreme Commander. In 1971, the Department of Defence became the Ministry of Defence (MoD-Abu Dhabi), and its head became the Minister of Defence, filled by Sheikh Khalifa.

The growth in capabilities of the ADDF's Sea and Air Wings meant they were increasingly given broader roles. Reflecting this role expansion, the Sea Wing formally became the ADDF Navy in 1971, and the Air Wing became the ADDF Air Force in 1972, although this change took a while to be operationalised. Further

Table 3: Leadership of the Abu Dhabi Defence Force	
Political head	**Executive commander**
Ruler: Sheikh Shakhbut bin Sultan Al Nahyan, Ruler of Abu Dhabi (r. 1928-1966) Sheikh Zayed bin Sultan Al Nahyan, Ruler of Abu Dhabi (r. 1966-2004), President of the UAE (1971-2004) **Delegated to:** Sheikh Khalifa bin Zayed Al Nahyan as Chairman of the Abu Dhabi Department of Defence (1969-1971), and as ADDF Commander-in-Chief (1974-1976)	**Commander ADDF** 1965-1969: Colonel E.B. (Tug) Wilson 1969-1971: Colonel J.T. (John) Paley 1971-1973: Brigadier General J.R.D. (Jake) Sharpe 1973: Colonel P. (Peter) MacDonald **Chief of Staff ADDF** 1973-mid-1970s: Brigadier General Sheikh Faisal bin Sultan Al Qasimi **Commander ADDF Land Forces** 1973-1976: Brigadier General R.J. (Ronald) Pope **Commander ADDF Air Wing/Air Force** 1969-1972: Lieutenant Colonel G.D. (Twinkle) Storey 1972-mid-1970s: Colonel M. Sadruddin **Commander ADDF Sea Wing/Navy** 1968-1973: Lieutenant Colonel Giles St G. Poole 1973-1975: Lieutenant Colonel E.E. (Peter) Pain 1975-1983: Brigadier General Mohammed Nabil Madhwar **Commander ADDF Emiri Guard** 1968-1970s: Colonel C.W. (Charles) Wontner 1970s: Lieutenant Colonel Obeid Rashid Al Arithi

An ADDF military parade in 1971. The men are wearing ceremonial summer uniform of terylene drill service dress with gray and white *shemagh*. The officer is wearing a Sam Browne belt with sword frog, grey lanyard and his *shemagh* is fringed and bobbled. The Warrant Officers and Senior NCOs are wearing a grey stable belt with the Force badge on the chrome buckle, a grey lanyard, and ceremonial sash. Black sandals were worn with parade dress in the force's early years. (Courtesy: UAE National Archives, 1971)

ADDF Ferret Scout Car, with the ADDF badge painted on the turret. Squadron commanders flew squadron pennants from their vehicles. These isosceles triangle-shaped pennants carried the squadron's colour with Arabic lettering. The armoured troops are wearing a gray and white *shemagh* on parade but otherwise wore a black beret. (Courtesy: UAE National Archives, c. 1971)

Colonel Edward "Tug" Wilson was the founder and first Commander of the ADDF. While in the Worcestershire Regiment, Wilson volunteered in 1961 for service with the Trucial Oman Scouts. In 1965 he was attached to the government of Abu Dhabi to raise and lead the ADDF. Wilson received the Order of the Star of Jordan, second grade from King Hussein in 1968, for his service in Abu Dhabi. He was replaced by Colonel John Paley in 1969. (Courtesy: UAE National Archives)

force structure changes were made in early December 1973. The ADDF was restructured into four commands – Land Forces, Air Force, Navy and Emiri Guard, and the posts of Commander and Deputy Commander ADDF were dissolved. All Abu Dhabi Ministries and Ministers were also abolished at this time as part of efforts to strengthen federation. The MoD-Abu Dhabi was renamed the Command of the General Headquarters (GHQ) of Abu Dhabi, headed up by the former Undersecretary of Defence, Brigadier General Sheikh Faisal bin Sultan Al Qasimi, who now carried the title of ADDF Chief of Staff. Sheikh Khalifa became the Commander-in-Chief of the ADDF.

In terms of the ADDF's command structure, the former HQ ADDF became the HQ ADDF Land Forces, with the Air Force, the Navy and Emiri Guard having their own headquarters. These technically reported separately to GHQ and the Commander-in-Chief. However, the actual arrangements appear to have varied with the force, time and scenario. For example, GHQ seems to have had very little influence over the Emiri Guard which was answerable directly to the Ruler. Another example was that during wartime, it was expected that the Commander Land Forces would assume command of all Abu Dhabi forces, with the Chief of Staff deploying to the field.

ADDF LAND FORCES

Land Forces formed a second infantry regiment (Sultan bin Zayed Regiment) around 1971, as well as the first armoured regiment

ADDF 25-pounder gun in 1971. (Courtesy: UAE National Archive)

(Salah ad-Din Regiment) and an artillery regiment (Hamdan bin Zayed Regiment). The force structure of the ADDF Land Forces around late 1973 was two Infantry Regiments (strength 743 men per regiment) each made up of an HQ and three Rifle Squadrons; an Armoured Car Regiment (strength approximately 600 men) made up of an HQ, four Squadrons, and a Vigilant anti-tank wire guided missile wing; and an Artillery Regiment (strength approximately 400 men) made up of an HQ and two batteries of nine 25-pounder howitzers.

By 1974, the Land Forces' combat units had become brigade-sized, and combat support units had become regiment-sized. In the first half of the 1970s, significant volumes of land forces equipment had been ordered and which started to arrive around the mid-1970s. This equipment included nearly 200 armoured personnel carriers, armoured cars, towed artillery guns, and surface to air missiles. It allowed the creation of mechanised infantry forces and improved offensive and defensive capabilities.

The first air defence battery was stood up in 1974, and by the end of the year it had grown into an Air Defence Regiment made up of three batteries and an HQ. Weapons consisted of 20mm AA guns and Rapier missiles.

The early 1970s also saw a significant enlargement in the ADDF's training infrastructure. New establishments included the 1971 founding of the Zayed Military Academy for officer cadets in Al Ain, and in 1974 in Mafraq, the establishment of the Armoured Centre, including an armoured school. Other training facilities were expanding, such as the Recruit Depot in Al Ain which had become a Training Regiment. The School of Infantry had also been established and by 1974 offered courses for NCOs, Troop Commanders and Squadron Commanders. New camps were built or existing ones upgraded. Support facilities were also developed, such as the Military Hospital (est. 1974), and weapons ranges.

By early 1973, the ADDF had an establishment strength of around 12,000 of which the vast bulk were Land Forces members. By early 1974, the ADDF was around 13,000 and by the 1976 unification of Emirati military forces, it was probably about 15,000.

ADDF/UAE AIR FORCE

By mid-1972, the Abu Dhabi Air Force's fleet had expanded by two additional Islanders, three SA.330 Puma medium transport/utility helicopters, and five Alouette III light utility helicopters. October 1973 was when the first of 30 Mirage supersonic strike-fighters arrived. These gave the force an air-to-air fighter capability and added to the force's clear-weather bombing attack strength. The additional aircraft based at the Al Bateen Air Base, coupled with an increase in civil aviation at that airport, resulted in the runways becoming increasingly congested. As a result, the Hunter Squadron was shifted to Sharjah airport in July 1973, and a few years later, the Mirages were rebased at Muqatara Air Base (now known as Al Dhafra Air Base) about 40km south-east of Al Bateen Airport.

To reflect the expansion of the Abu Dhabi Air Force's capability, it was renamed the UAE Air Force in 1974. By April 1974, it consisted of an HQ, three Squadrons, two Flights plus a movements (i.e. flight management) and radar unit.

Staffed by Pakistani personnel, the 1st Squadron operated up to 12 Mirage 5AD strike-fighters and two 5DAD two-seat combat trainers. The second Squadron was made up of 10 Hunters (eight FGA.76 single seat and two T.77 two-seat trainers as two had been lost in accidents). The third Squadron was made up of five Pumas and five Alouette III helicopters. The transport aircraft were organized into two flights. One was made up of four Caribous and the other of five Islanders. Both transport and communications aircraft numbers would continue to grow and by 1975, they consisted of a Skyvan 3M 19-seat light transport aircraft, three more SA330 Pumas, two C130H Hercules long-range transports, a number of Alouette III helicopters, and the first two of four Bell 205A-1 tactical troop-carrying helicopters.

While in the late 1960s, the overwhelming majority of pilots and other air officers were British, this changed in the early 1970s. Increasing numbers of pilot posts were filled by seconded Sudanese, Jordanian and Pakistani officers, and by late 1973, the majority of air force officers were Pakistanis. Up until 1972, the commander of Abu Dhabi's air forces was a British contracted officer. He was

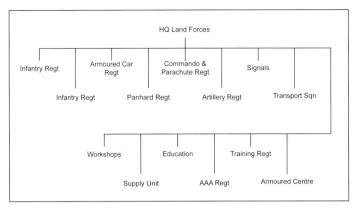

Figure 4: Structure of the Abu Dhabi Land Forces, 1974.

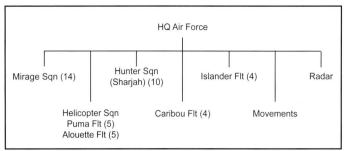

Figure 5: Structure of Abu Dhabi Air Force, 1974.

replaced by a seconded Pakistan Air Force officer, and Pakistanis would continue to command the nation's air force until the early 1980s.

ADDF/UAE NAVY

Between 1971, when the ADDF Sea Wing was re-designated as the ADDF Navy, and 1976 when all Emirati forces were integrated into the UAE Armed Forces and the force was re-designated as the UAE Navy, the only new naval combat vessels introduced were six 110ft large patrol craft, built by Vosper Thornycroft. Armed with two 30mm twin cannons and one 20mm cannon, these craft were introduced in 1975 and 1976. In 1974 and 1975, it also received five 9m inshore patrol craft.

During these years, the naval forces' infrastructure improved considerably. In 1973, a forward operations facility was created at

ADDF Saladin Armoured Car in 1971. The commander is wearing a black beret with the ADDF headdress badge. (Courtesy: UAE National Archives)

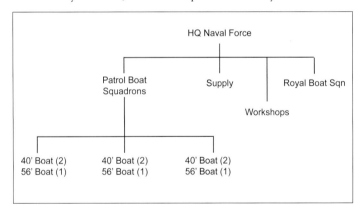

Figure 6: Structure of Abu Dhabi Navy, 1974

the far west of the Abu Dhabi coast at Dohat Al Quwaisat, and another constructed at Khor Fakkan in Sharjah Emirate on the Gulf of Oman. In 1975, the main naval base was moved from near the Al Nahyan camp where access was restricted during low tide to a new naval base at the new deep-water Abu Dhabi port.

Old British 6-pounder anti-tank guns used as Saluting Guns by the ADDF. (Courtesy: Alastair MacDonald)

Reviewing a parade in 1973. Left to right: Lieutenant General Sheikh Khalifa Bin Zayed Al Nahyan, Commander-in-Chief, ADDF; Sheikh Zayed Bin Sultan Al Nahyan, President of the UAE, Ruler of Abu Dhabi and Supreme Commander of the ADDF; Awadh Mohammed Al Khalidi, a Jordanian seconded officer who would become the first Chief of Staff of the UAE Armed Forces in 1976. (Courtesy: UAE National Archives, c. 1973)

ADDF parade celebrating the 5th Anniversary of Sheikh Zayed bin Sultan Al Nahyan's accession as Ruler of Abu Dhabi. (Courtesy: UAE National Archives, 1971)

The P402 *Ghadunfar* was one of the six 40 foot *Dhafeer* class coastal patrol boats which arrived between mid-1968 and mid-1970. These were the first combat vessels of the Sea Wing of the ADDF. With a range of 350 nautical miles at 15 knots, the boats enabled Abu Dhabi to start patrolling its own and other Emirates' waters. These vessels were armed with a 0.5" heavy machine gun and two 0.303" Bren light machine guns on the flying bridge. (Courtesy: UAE National Archives, c. 1971)

An ADDF naval officer wearing the working dress (*mazri* cotton) shirt worn by all ADDF personnel. It is the colour of the red sands in Abu Dhabi's western desert. Until the early 1970s, naval officers wore British naval ranks. The Sea Wing officers at this time wore the Royal Navy white topped cap with the ADDF headdress badge. This was later replaced by the ADDF *shemagh* when Abu Dhabi's naval force subsequently adopted army ranks, and the insignia was duly altered to reflect this. In this photo, Captain (army rank) D. Gregory is wearing the grey ADDF stable belt with chrome buckle and ADDF badge. (Courtesy: David Gregory, c. 1971)

In 1975, the UAE Navy had a strength of some 400 personnel, the majority of whom were expatriates. In the first few years of the ADDF Sea Wing, contracted British officers dominated the officer corps. By 1976, they had mostly been replaced by Egyptians and Pakistani seconded officers. Ratings were mostly Omani with technical posts primarily filled by Pakistanis.

The organisational structure during this period consisted of a small HQ, one Patrol Boat Squadron, the Royal Boat Squadron (i.e. the Ruler's yachts), and workshop and supply groups. The Patrol Boat Squadron was made up of three Divisions, each of which consisted of one 56ft and two 40ft patrol boats.

Desert Wolves, the popular name of the Majmooh Tariq bin Ziyad (Tariq bin Ziyad Group) 1971. The heritage of the Desert Wolves started with the formation in 1970 of 9 Squadron ADDF which was redesignated in November 1970 as the Force HQ Defence Squadron. In 1971 it was renamed the Tariq bin Ziyad Group. (Courtesy: UAE National Archives)

4

DUBAI DEFENCE FORCE

In 1970, the Ruler of Dubai, Sheikh Rashid bin Saeed Al Maktoum, ordered the formation of a military force. The rationale for its formation was to provide protection for the emirate at a time when it was uncertain whether a federation of emirates would be established when the British departed at the end of the year. The rapidly growing Abu Dhabi Defence Force was also a concern.

The first commander of the Dubai Defence Force (DDF) was Captain Keith Steel, a 27-year old TOS officer detached to the DDF. He arrived in February 1971 and at an operational level, took instructions from both Sheikh Mohammed bin Rashid Al Maktoum, the third son of the Dubai Ruler and the head of Dubai Police, and Dubai Police's executive commander, Jack Briggs. Before Captain Steel's arrival, these two had already decided on the structure of the force and ordered its weapons, radios and vehicles. Captain Steel was tasked to build a force of 400 to 500 soldiers.

In addition to Captain Steel, the TOS detached one of its Arab officers and a number of NCOs to assist him. In mid-1971, a small Jordanian military team arrived to support recruit training, but it was not effective and soon terminated. To provide a base of experienced soldiers for the DDF, the TOS allowed its serving Dubai citizens to resign and join the nascent force. Other initial recruits were the armed retainers of the Ruler.

Sheikh Rashid wanted his force to be predominately Dubai citizens or citizens of other Emirates, rather than foreign nationals. This meant the force grew more slowly than the Abu Dhabi military.

By 1973, three 150-man Rifle Squadrons had been raised. Each Rifle Squadron in the DDF had three Troops. Every Troop had sufficient Land Rovers to carry the entire Troop on patrol or into action. The G3 rifle initially issued was later replaced with the SLR. As the force was growing towards regimental strength, Dubai requested a senior serving regimental officer from Britain to command the force. Thus from 1972, Lieutenant Colonel A.B. (Tony) Wallerstein became Commander DDF. In 1974 he was replaced by another seconded British officer, Colonel Michael Barclay, who led the DDF until 1976, when he handed command over to the first Emirati commander, Sheikh Colonel Ahmed bin Rashid Al Maktoum, the fourth son of the Dubai Ruler.

With the arrival of Saladin armoured cars and Ferret scout cars in 1972, an armoured car squadron of eight Ferrets and eight (later 18) Saladins was established. An Emiri Guard force had also been established by this time, made up of both a plain-clothes mobile guard and uniformed static palace guards. The DDF had access to helicopter and light aircraft support through the Dubai Police Air Wing, which was administered by the police but was under the direct command of Sheikh Mohammed bin Rashid in his capacity as head of the Dubai Police and DDF. The Air Wing served both the police and the DDF. Initially, its commander and pilots were all Western expatriates, but from 1974, Dubai nationals started to serve as pilots.

On 20 August 1973, a dispute over land ownership at Tawi Nizwa on the Sharjah-Dubai border escalated into an exchange of shots between the forces of the two emirates, and included shots being fired at a DDF helicopter which carried the force's Commanding Officer Lieutenant Colonel Wallerstein. While the personal intervention of the UAE President, Sheikh Zayed, calmed the situation, this incident partly explains the DDF's expansion in the mid-1970s. In 1974 and 1975, equipment to arrive included Scorpion armoured

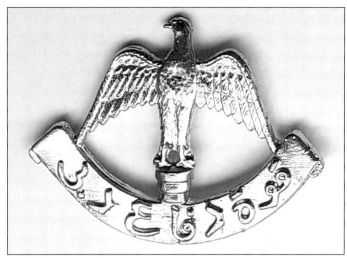

A DDF headdress badge. The headdress badge depicted a falcon with outstretched wings on a plinth, with the Arabic script under it reading 'Dubai Defence Force'. (Authors' collection)

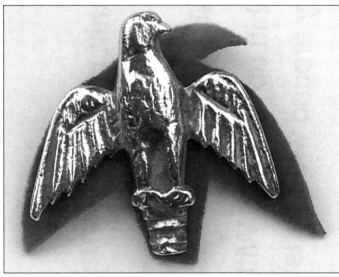

The rank badge of a major of the DDF, on the red velvet backing placed on epaulets. (Courtesy: Miles Stockwell)

A DDF silver button worn by officers. These came in two sizes–larger ones for the tunic and smaller ones for epaulets. (Courtesy: Miles Stockwell)

1 Rifle Squadron DDF Commanders LWB FFR Land Rover. (Courtesy: Keith Steel)

Sheikh Mohammad bin Rashid Al Maktoum wearing the uniform of the DDF, 1971-1972. At that time, he was UAE Minister of Defence and head of both Dubai's police and military forces. While initially the DDF wore a blue/grey *mazri* jacket similar to the TOS, this was rapidly replaced by the beige jacket in this photograph, and khaki long trousers. Sheikh Mohammad is also wearing the red and white chequered *shemagh* with black *agal*. Officers and Warrant Officers wore British officer peaked hats, the Armoured Car Squadron wore black berets and HQ Squadron wore red berets. No collar badges were worn. (Courtesy: Keith Steel)

The founding commander of the DDF, Captain Keith Steel, who was detached from the TOS to form the force and is seen wearing TOS insignia. After 1971, he continued to command the DDF but as a seconded British officer. (Courtesy: Keith Steel)

DDF officers, c. 1974-1975. Front, left to right: Major Miles Stockwell, OC A Squadron; Captain Sheikh Ahmed Maktoum Al Maktoum, 2IC A Squadron, Lieutenant Sheikh Mohammed Obaid Al Maktoum 2IC B Squadron. In the background: Lieutenant Juma wears the black beret of the Armoured Car Squadron. A DDF Saladin armoured car can also be seen. Rank insignia for officers is worn on epaulets. The metal belt buckle carries the DDF motif. (Courtesy: Miles Stockwell)

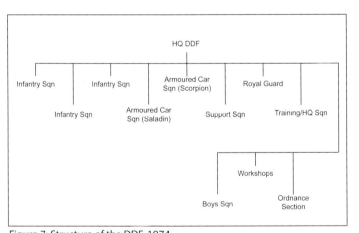

Figure 7: Structure of the DDF, 1974

reconnaissance tracked vehicles, 81mm mortars, 20mm Hispano-Suiza anti-aircraft weapons, 84mm Carl Gustav anti-tank recoilless rifles, Bedford trucks, Scammel trucks and GPMGs.

By the end of 1974, the DDF consisted of an HQ, three infantry squadrons, two armoured car squadrons (one made up of 18 Saladins and four Ferret scout cars, and the other with 10 tracked Scorpion reconnaissance vehicles and four Ferrets), and a support squadron (equipped with 81mm mortars and 20mm AA cannons). It also had an Emiri Guard, and support units in the form of a signal squadron, training squadron, ordnance squadron, workshops and a boys' training squadron. By 1975, the total strength of the DDF was 1,733

personnel. More Scorpions were delivered in that year, allowing an armoured regiment to be established in 1976, along with a second infantry regiment. Vehicles sported squadron pennants. Each rifle squadron commander's Land Rover had a light blue pennant with a white Arabic number. A pipe band also existed, which was similar to the former TOS band.

In 1974 and 1975, the Dubai Police Air Wing received additional aircraft, bringing its fleet of helicopters to two troop-transporting Augusta Bell 205A-1s, three light Augusta Bell 206Bs, one Cessna 182 and one Siai-Marchetti SF.260WD Warrior piston engine trainer. 1975 also saw a major new capability introduced to the DDF – ground-attack aircraft. Four Aeromacchi MB-326G jet trainer/ light ground-attack aircraft arrived, three were MB-326KD single-seat ground-attack aircraft, and one was a MB-326LD two-seat advanced jet trainer. These new aircraft resulted in the Air Wing taking on new military significance, and it became more of a light air force. By this time, the DDF had a range of bases across the emirate, including a new DDF headquarters at Jumeirah, a training centre at Al Aweer about 30 km from Dubai, a training camp in the Hatta enclave on the Oman border, and a camp at Jebel Ali.

In 1976, the DDF was renamed the Central Military Command and became one of the three regional commands within the now unified UAE Armed Forces.

Table 4: Leadership of the Dubai Defence Force	
Political head	**Executive commander**
Ruler:	1970-1972: Captain K. (Keith) Steel
Sheikh Rashid bin Saeed Al Maktoum (r. 1958-1990)	1972-1974: Lieutenant Colonel A.B. (Tony) Wallerstein
Delegated to:	1974-1976: Colonel M. L. (Michael) Barclay
Sheikh Mohammad bin Rashid Al Maktoum as Head of Police and Public Security	1976-?: Colonel Sheikh Ahmed bin Rashid Al Maktoum

5
ABU DHABI POLICE

The official establishment date of the Abu Dhabi Police was 1957, however the first attempt to form a local gendarme force dates to 1954. This was when the Ruler of Abu Dhabi, Sheikh Shakhbut bin Sultan Al Nahyan, ordered the formation of a security force following concerns that he was facing a foreign-sponsored takeover. Guards were hired to man small fortifications that controlled or monitored entry onto Abu Dhabi Island, and night patrols of Abu Dhabi town were instigated. Two hundred rifles were purchased to arm the force. While the coup attempt never materialised, the Ruler recognised the need for a more professional security force rather than the traditional tribal armed guards and retainers. Given the absence of professional security experience by local citizens, the Ruler requested training from the TOL.

The TOL agreed, and in April 1955 started training a local force at Al Maqta Fort in Abu Dhabi. However, this training ended in September 1955 after the trainees stopped attending because they had not been paid by the Ruler. The Ruler was notoriously reluctant to part with money, and consequently the force dissolved and the TOL detachment departed.

A second attempt was made by the Ruler in 1957 to professionalise his force, now known as the Abu Dhabi Police. At this time, the force numbered some 80 men, was commanded by the Ruler's son, Sheikh Sultan, and had three key roles. The first was to escort the Ruler and senior family sheikhs, notably his brother Sheikh Zayed, the governor of Al Ain, and to guard their palaces. The second was to guard oil camps in the Emirate's hinterland as Western companies explored for oil and – following the 1958 discovery of oil in commercial quantities – built oil extraction and export facilities. The third was to man checkpoints, notably on Abu Dhabi Island and in Al Ain, to identify who was entering the area. The Ruler paid for the police (rather than the British as in Dubai) although he charged the oil companies for the police posts associated with their camps.

In early 1957, the Ruler again asked for British assistance in training the force and by later that year, it had provided arms and started training NCOs from the Abu Dhabi Police at its training centre near Sharjah. Sheikh Sultan attended a TOS training course, and carried the rank of Staff Sergeant.

Sheikh Shakhbut recognised the limitations of having a police force run by NCOs rather than officers, and consequently asked the British to find a British police officer to lead his force. In March 1959, a Briton who had colonial policing experiencing in India and Sudan, Mr Crosby Stokes, was appointed as the commander. Consequently, Staff Sergeant Sheikh Sultan withdrew from the police.

During 1959, police strength increased to several hundred, with most being stationed in Abu Dhabi and Al Ain. The reason for the

Abu Dhabi Police 1971 headdress badge based on a falcon which symbolises royalty, force and courage. The falcon sits on crossed daggers (*khunjars*), and the Arabic script underneath reads 'Security'. Below are collar badges were worn on some orders of dress, possibly only by officers. (Courtesy: Abu Dhabi Police)

A member of the Abu Dhabi Police, 1957. Normally the cap badge has the member's police number but it is absent in this photo. He is wearing an orange *shemagh* which had a light pattern of browns and white at the edges. (Courtesy: Abu Dhabi Police)

An Abu Dhabi Police unit on Das Island during the mid to late-1950s. The uniform consists of khaki shirts and trousers. (Courtesy: Abu Dhabi Police)

Sheikh Shakhbut, Ruler of Abu Dhabi, reviewing an Abu Dhabi Police parade. In the background is the Abu Dhabi flag. (Courtesy: Abu Dhabi Police, early to mid-1960s)

expansion in the force numbers was to guard the growing number of the Ruler's buildings, customs offices, markets and banks. The force had also expanded its posts in the hinterland. The most significant, geopolitically, was the post in Abu Dhabi's far west, on the south shore of the Khor Al Odaid inlet. Established in October 1958, the location of the post was selected to show neighbouring states that all the land to the east belonged to Abu Dhabi. The post's location raised tensions with both Qatar and Saudi Arabia, as the boundary between Abu Dhabi Emirate and their domains had never been formalised and remained contested. To further assert Abu Dhabi's control over fishing rights in the area, a launch was stationed at the police post to stop the entry of Qatari launches. This led to occasional exchanges of gun fire between the Abu Dhabi police post and Qatari police during the year, with the dispute eventually settled through a unilateral decision by Britain about the location of the

borders. While Sheikh Shakhbut rejected the British-determined border location as he believed that some of the land given to Qatar actually belonged to Abu Dhabi, he was powerless to do anything about the British decision due to the treaty arrangements between Abu Dhabi and Britain.

By early 1961, the Abu Dhabi Police had reached a strength of 255 men. Its command structure consisted of the British commander with an Arab officer as second-in-command. It had no specialised branches, but maintained a small prison. A British review of the force at that time stated that it was reasonably equipped with vehicles and weapons, and had a sea-going launch. Despite this, it noted that the funding of the force was an issue. Rather than providing the force with a budget, the Ruler required that every expenditure obtain his personal approval, even those as small as repairs for a policeman's boot. This, along with his sometimes parsimonious and

Abu Dhabi Police standing guard at Qasr Al Hosn, the Ruler's fort on Abu Dhabi Island, 1966. (Courtesy: UAE National Archives)

Abu Dhabi Police on parade, 1969. The policeman is wearing the Abu Dhabi Police 1971 headdress badge on his beret, and silver collar badges consisting of individual gazelles facing one another on black cloth. The policeman's white metal number is clearly visible on the black cloth backing. Around the time of the formation of the Department of Police and Public Security in 1966-1967, police started to wear a black and white chequered *shemagh* with traffic police wearing a white *shemagh* or black beret. Otherwise, the uniform was similar to that of the previous organisation. (Courtesy: UAE National Archives):

capricious behaviour, constrained the force's development. Pay was often multiple months in arrears. This reduced the attractiveness of employment with the police compared to the Trucial Oman Scouts or the oil companies, which had an effect on both the quality and quantity of recruits. Morale in the force was low and retention was an ongoing problem. Training was often negligible.

A significant step forward in the professionalisation of the force began in 1960, when Abu Dhabi Police personnel started to attend specialised police training institutions in the region. Initially, four police officers were sent to Kuwait in December of that year.

In 1961, the force's leadership changed when Sheikh Shakhbut did not renew Mr Stokes' contract. Another British police office, Mr Bill Edge, was recruited to head the force. He arrived in March 1961 and was given the rank of Lieutenant Colonel. His deputy was Sheikh Mubarak bin Mohammed Al Nahyan, a cousin of the Ruler.

Upon arrival in March 1961, Lieutenant Colonel Edge was instructed by the Ruler to increase the size of the force and to make them more "soldier-like". This probably reflected a desire to build a better armed and trained protection force. Lieutenant Colonel Edge recommended a number of changes to the police which were agreed to by the Ruler. But within months, the Ruler had changed his mind stating he did not wish to spend so much money on the police. Consequently, the capabilities and structure of the police did not change markedly.

However, the need for improvements became obvious during a series of strikes and disturbances in mid-1963 at oil camps in Jebel Dhanna, Tarif and on Das Island. These disturbances resulted in a number of injuries, including injuries to Americans and Europeans who managed and provided the skilled labour at the camps. The local police posts were unable to maintain order, and calm returned only after the intervention of the Ruler's local representatives and the TOS. By stopping the immediate flow of oil, these disturbances had the potential to seriously interrupt the source of the Ruler's wealth–oil exports. They also endangered development plans, as the regional US Government representative told Sheikh Shakhbut that US nationals at the camps would leave if security did not improve.

Sheikh Shakhbut once again recognised the need to have more professional personnel and to improve the force's standards of discipline, leadership and shooting. The British recommended bringing in external support, and in July 1963 the Ruler agreed to accept a seconded police officer from Bahrain for three months, and the attachment to the police of one British and three Arab sergeants from the TOS for a similar period. However, shortly afterwards, he reversed this last decision due to an unwillingness to pay the salaries. One British officer did arrive. Around October 1963, the Bahraini Police officer, Assistant Superintendent Parrett, arrived in Abu Dhabi to build a riot squad. This had a short-term benefit, but following his departure the squad was dispersed and the capability evaporated.

Thus by 1964, there had been no fundamental change to the Abu Dhabi Police, except that it was slightly larger at around 300 men.

An ongoing weakness of the Abu Dhabi Police was that the police remained static at its posts rather than patrolling the area around them. This meant the police had limited ability to control entry onto Abu Dhabi Island and across borders as those seeking to enter

Ferret Scout Cars were operated by three Emirati forces, the ADDF, DDF, and RAKMF. The markings varied from one to another. The above image is of an ADDF Ferret. Included is the ADDF insignia (similar to the cap badge), and a red and white square TAC sign with the red half as the top part of the diagonal. They also had white vehicle numbers on a black background applied on the front of the vehicle. (Artwork by David Bocquelet)

The ADDF acquired a total of 20 Saracen armoured personnel carriers, which had a crew of two and could carry up to nine troops. Their armament varied but typically included a medium machine gun in the turret, and a light machine gun. They received a two tone camouflage pattern – like some of the ADDF's Saladin armoured cars. (Artwork by David Bocquelet)

The ADDF, DDF and UDF all acquired and used Saladin armoured cars over time. In the case of the ADDF, both the Salah ad-Din and Khalifa bin Zayed regiments were equipped with the type which had a 76mm L5A1 gun as its primary armament. Secondary armament included two medium machine guns. The number plate is in black and the red shield indicates the vehicle belongs to the Emiri Guard. In 1973-1974, six of the ADDF's Saladins were loaned – together with their crews – to the Sultan of Oman's Armed Forces in support of the ongoing counterinsurgency effort. (Artwork by David Bocquelet)

This Land Rover Series 2 SWB is shown flying an ADDF pennant from its right fender. As usual, the vehicle was painted in sand overall. Each rifle squadron of the force, and all the supporting units, were equipped with this type of general utility vehicle. (Artwork by David Bocquelet)

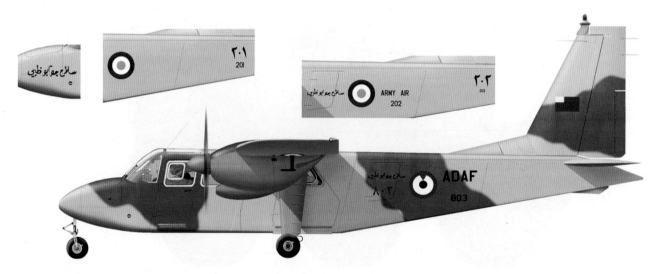

The first two Britten-Norman BN-2 Islanders of the ADAF wore a livery consisting of beige (BS381C/388) overall, with undersurfaces in light admiralty grey (BS381C/697). Applied in black, their service titles were distributed as shown inset in the upper left corner, on the nose and the rear fuselage – before being 'grouped' around the roundel in the 1971-1972 period. By the mid-1970s, the aircraft had received a camouflage pattern consisting of dark brown (BS381C/411) atop of beige, while undersurfaces were painted in aircraft blue (BS381C/108) or cobalt blue (BS381C/115). Except for early during their service, fin-flashes were always worn, and roundels were applied in six positions. (Artwork by Tom Cooper).

Two Augusta-Bell AB 206 Jet Rangers were the first helicopters acquired by Abu Dhabi for its Air Wing in the early 1970s. While there are reports that at least one received a camouflage pattern in the form of dark green or dark brown atop the overall yellow-sand, all colour photographs show them painted in yellow sand only. National insignia and service titles were applied at the rear of the fuselage. All Jet Rangers were transferred to the UDF in around 1973, and operated from Dubai airport. (Artwork by Tom Cooper)

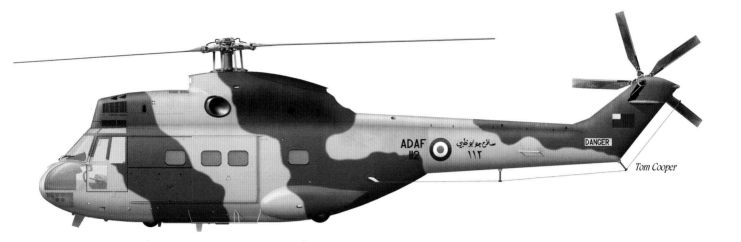

Abu Dhabi placed an order for three Aerospatiale SA.330C Pumas to supplement Jet Rangers of the Helicopter Flight in 1972. The camouflage scheme of the Pumas in the UAE is uncertain but when they left France they had all received a wraparound camouflage pattern consisting of Brun Café (light sand) and Brun Noisette (dark earth) colours. All inscriptions – including the service title and serial in English, on one side of the roundel, and the same but in Arabic, on the other – were in black. The sole exception was the warning insignia on the fin, applied in white. The ADAF's Pumas received tinted cockpit and cabin windows. (Artwork by Tom Cooper)

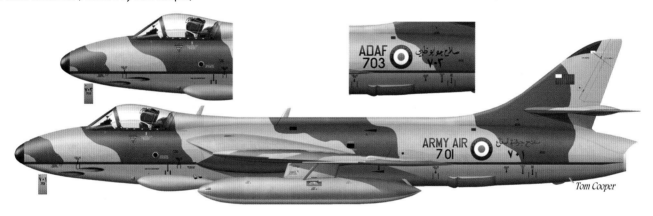

The initial combat element of the ADDF's Air Wing was a squadron equipped with refurbished Hawker Hunter fighter-bombers, ordered through the Contract No. HAS/69//AD/082, in February 1969. This consisted of seven FGA.Mk 76 fighter-bombers (serials 701-707), three FR.Mk 76A single-seat reconnaissance fighters (serials 708-710), and two T.Mk 77 two-seat conversion trainers (serials 711-712). All were painted in light stone and dark brown on upper surfaces and sides: at least the first two FGA.Mk 76s – possibly the first FR.Mk 76A, too – had their undersides painted in light admiralty grey: subsequent examples received a coat of either aircraft blue (BS381C/108) or cobalt blue (BS381C/115) instead. Initially home-based at Abu Dhabi's Al Bateen Airport, what was originally known just as Hunter Squadron was re-designated to the I Shaheen Squadron and re-deployed to Sharjah, in the mid-1970s. Except for two FR.Mk 76As lost in accidents (708 and 710), and one T.Mk 77 that was broken down for spares, surviving examples were subsequently donated to Somalia. (Artwork by Tom Cooper)

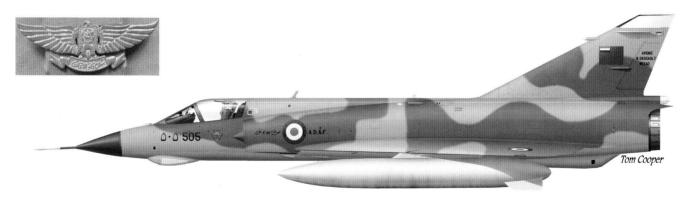

In 1972, the ADDF's Air Wing was expanded into the Abu Dhabi Air Force. Following an evaluation of a number of competitive multi-role fighters – including the BAe Harrier and the Northrop F-5E Tiger II – the Abu Dhabi Air Force opted for the Dassault Mirage 5. Initial order included 12 Mirage 5AD fighter-bombers, 2 two-seat Mirage 5DAD conversion-trainers (serials 201 and 203), and two Mirage 5RAD reconnaissance fighters (serials 601 and 603). Delivered in 1974-1975, they were all operated by Pakistani personnel of the II Shaheen Squadron from Abu Dhabi's Al Bateen Airport, then Al Dhafra Air Base. A follow-up order in 1974 added 14 Mirage 5EAD interceptors (serials 501-5014), one of which is shown here in its original camouflage pattern and markings: the former consisted of French colours Brun Café and Kaki on top surfaces and sides, and Gris Bleu Clair on under surfaces. Inset is shown the badge of the Union Air Force. The scroll on the badge states Union Air Force. (Artwork by Tom Cooper)

Top left: The Trucial Oman Scouts bandsmen wore white tropical uniforms and red and white chequered *shemagh* with black *agul*, which had a single silver *khunjah* badge with pin fitting attached. Brass shoulder titles in Arabic script were worn, together with red ceremonial lanyards, and a red stable belt with brown leather fastening to the front, and black leather sandals. The TOS Ceremonial Troop carried a dark green guidon with gold embroidered crossed *khunjahs* on a scroll. Officers had their lanyards on the right shoulder. (Artwork by Anderson Subtil)

Right: An ADDF commando from the Desert Wolves commando unit, established in 1971. He is shown wearing a Commando Green beret with ADDF badge, and a sand-coloured cravat that could be worn around his head when on patrol, '*shemagh*' fashion'. British-made, Disruptive Pattern Material (DPM) camouflage uniforms were issued along with British 1944-pattern style belts and Bata suede desert boots. The weapon carried is a Sterling sub machine gun. (Artwork by Anderson Subtil)

Bottom: An officer of the TOS shown as during field operations, wearing a red and white chequered *shemagh* with a black *agal* and silver officers' TOS headdress badge attached. A grey/blue jacket was worn with silver buttons that had the TOS emblem on them. Brass TOS shoulder titles were also worn. Webbing was of British 1937 pattern, while a red lanyard was worn on the right shoulder, 'officer style'. Khaki long trousers were worn in combination with Bata suede desert boots. (Artwork by Anderson Subtil)

Headdress badges of Emirati forces (from left to right). Abu Dhabi Police, 1971-1974; Abu Dhabi Police 1968-1971; Abu Dhabi Police 1957-1967; Sharjah Police; Ras Al Khaimah Mobile Force; and Dubai Defence Force (Courtesy: Abu Dhabi Police and Cliff Lord collection)

The various epaulets, shoulder titles, rank insignia and patches worn by Abu Dhabi Police over the decades. (Courtesy: Abu Dhabi Police)

Evolution of Abu Dhabi/UAE Armed Forces signal badges, from 1970 until present (from left to right): three ADDF signal force badges, each with different border colours (yellow: 1st grade; blue: 2nd grade; and red: 3rd grade); UAE Signal Corps cloth patch (1976-present); and two cloth patches of ADDF signals (used 1974-1975). (Courtesy: UAE Signal Corps)

From left to right: shoulder badges of an ADDF Sea Wing naval lieutenant (the ADDF Sea Wing used army ranks and this rank was referred to as Captain); ADDF Emir's Guard shoulder badge; C Squadron commander's pennants used by the TOS and the UDF; and E Squadron commander's pennant of the UDF. (Courtesy: David Gregory, Cliff Lord, Nick Weeks, and William Naesmyth)

ADDF Al Dhafrah Brigade

UAE Air Defence

UAE Al Badr Brigade

UAE Al Dhafrah Brigade

UAE Artillery

UAE Para

UAE Transport Logistics and Supply

UAE Basic Training Regt

UAE Chemical Defence

UAE EME

UAE Field Engineers

UAE Medical Services

UAE Signals

Various Abu Dhabi/UAE Armed Forces cloth unit insignias. The early ADDF insignia in 1970s, formed the basis for many of the later UAE insignia. For instance, the ADDFs Al Dhafrah Brigade's patch is similar to the UAE's Al Dhafra Brigade. (Courtesy: Cliff Lord)

Badges of the Federal Armed Forces from 1974 and worn by the UDF. Left to right: Brass coloured headdress badge, officers pip rank insignia, major shoulder insignia, silver collar badge (police) and gold land force badge. Note the Police were issued with the same badges at this time but in silver. The badges were replaced in the early 1980s. (Courtesy: Cliff Lord)

Headdress badges of several Emirates (L to R): Abu Dhabi Police 1968-1971 also in silver with enamelled flags in red and white, (collar badges of silver gazelle facing inwards worn by all ranks), Ajman Police in silver and enamelled flag, Fujairah Police, Sharjah National Guard officers silver badge, Umm al Quwain Defence Force. (Courtesy: Cliff Lord)

Emirati military forces (from left to right): headdress badge of the ADDF (dull type). Arabic script reads 'Abu Dhabi Defence Force'; UAE Major's anodized aluminium rank insignia replacing ADDF and UDF major rank badges from around 1973; ADDF silver collar badge for shirts: ADDF pip rank badge and aluminium shoulder title which reads Abu Dhabi Defence Force. (Courtesy: Cliff Lord)

An element of an ADDF rifle squadron forming up for a desert exercise, c. 1972. Eight soldiers with their weapons could be squeezed into the long wheel-base Land Rovers in the picture. The troops are wearing working dress–khaki drill shirt and trousers, British 1944 pattern webbing, grey and white *shemagh* with a black *agal* and headdress badge, and desert boots. Normally the grey lanyard was worn in the field. They are armed with SLRs. (Courtesy: Tim Cooper)

An ADDF Land Rover Series 2, with senior officer, during a public parade around 1970. The vehicle had an ADDF flag flying from the right wing. Visible below is the TAC sign and then the registration number. On the left side was the ADDF emblem and below it the white saltire cross on a red background. (Courtesy: Alastair MacDonald)

The various shirts of the TOS, late 1960s. The British NCO on the left is wearing a faded blue-grey shirt tucked in, the Arab officer in the centre is wearing a bush jacket with silver buttons, and the British NCO on the left is wearing the blue-grey shirt pulled out summer style. Officers and Warrant Officers wore a red lanyard on the right shoulder with all others wearing it on their left. (Courtesy: William Naesmyth)

A good view of typical tactical signs as applied on a Land Rover of the TOS' Support Group in the late 1960s. These were also carried on front surfaces, and included the TOS symbol (white disc with a single red dagger), and the squadron or unit sign (the latter included a diagonally divided red and white square for the FHQ; red triangle for A Squadron; red square for B Squadron; red circle for C Squadron; red vertical oblong non-voided for D Squadron; red D for E Squadron; black saltire cross on a yellow square for X Squadron; red flash for the Signal Squadron; red crescent for the Medical Unit; red diamond outline with red steering wheel in the centre for the Motor Transport Squadron; red machine gun tactical symbol for the Support Group, and crossed hammers and tongs for the Workshops). (Courtesy: Miles Stockwell)

Abu Dhabi Police detachment with a blue Toyota long wheelbase, 2-wheel drive FJ42 Land Cruiser at al-Maqta Customs and Police Post, as of around 1968. The latter controlled entry to Abu Dhabi Island. (Courtesy: Abu Dhabi Police)

A Land Rover of the UDF's E Squadron with packs hanging off the side of the vehicle to make room for soldiers in the back, early 1970s. The photo shows that the UDF's TAC signs remained those of the TOS. E Squadron's TAC sign was a lazy D (a letter D on its back). Vehicle TAC signs were used until around 1974. On the right hand side can be seen a white disc with the red sign of the UDF similar to the cap badge. Later the red TOS-era signs became black. (Courtesy: William Naesmyth)

One of 12 Mirage 5AD fighter-bombers ordered in 1972 and delivered in 1974. The camouflage pattern consisted of Brun Café and Kaki on top surfaces. (Courtesy: Tom Cooper Collection)

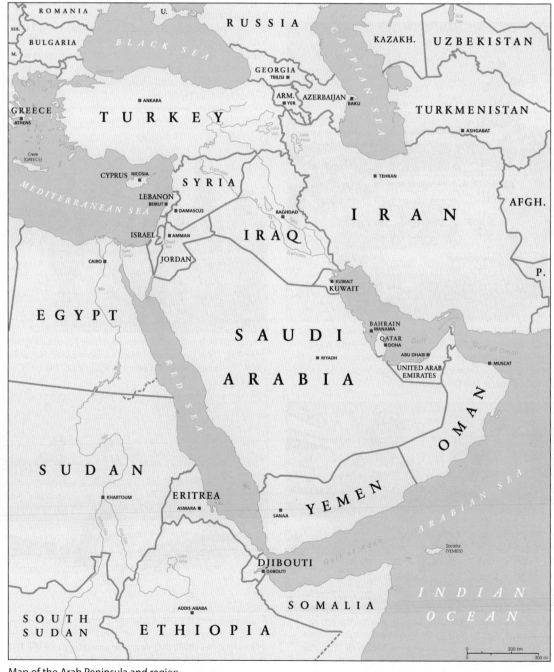

Map of the Arab Peninsula and region.

Recruit graduation parade of the Abu Dhabi Police, 1969. (Courtesy: UAE National Archives)

Abu Dhabi Police Force graduation, 1969. (Courtesy: UAE National Archives)

surreptitiously could go around the posts. Another limitation was that the police had no mobile reserve, let alone a riot-trained one, so if trouble occurred in the oil fields, sizeable reinforcements could not be sent quickly. Also, just as in the past, salaries were unpaid for months at a time, and morale and retention continued to be a problem. By 1964, the Ruler had lost confidence in Lieutenant Colonel Edge and made Sheikh Mubarak bin Muhammad the commander of the Police with Lieutenant Colonel Edge remaining on in an advisory role.

In August 1966, Sheikh Zayed replaced his brother as Ruler of Abu Dhabi, which was to have a profound effect on the police. Sheikh Zayed had long advocated for the need to modernise the Emirate's system of government, such as establishing departments with budgets, delegating authority to departmental heads and bringing in foreign expertise to rapidly develop capability.

Consequently, by the end of that year, he had established

Traffic officer of the Abu Dhabi Police Force, 1970s. (Courtesy: UAE National Archives)

Abu Dhabi Police collar badges, as worn in the period 1968-1971. (Authors' collection)

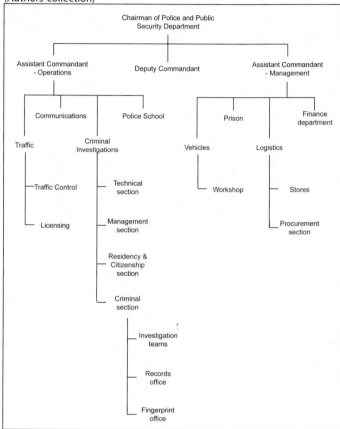

Figure 8: Structure for the Abu Dhabi Police, c. 1967.

administrative arrangements to create an Abu Dhabi government. This included creating the Police and Public Security Department which oversaw Abu Dhabi Police. The Chairman of the Department was Colonel Sheikh Mubarak bin Mohammed who remained Commandant of Abu Dhabi Police. He was supported by a deputy commander for police operations and administration.

The next two years saw the police evolve into a modern force made up of specialised branches including Marine, Traffic, Criminal Investigation and Special Branch. To build the new organisation, small numbers of experienced British police personnel were engaged in late 1966 and early 1967, including Mr A.S. (Stacey) Barham who became Deputy Commandant. These experienced personnel established and administered specialised functions, including traffic, workshops and communications. In 1968, the first large team of

seconded Jordanian police personnel arrived to assist in building and staffing new functions. Jordanian secondees would continue to be provided until 1979. 1968 also saw the establishment of the Abu Dhabi Police School, which was followed in 1969 by the Police College which graduated officers. A Communications School was also formed around this time. The force grew significantly from

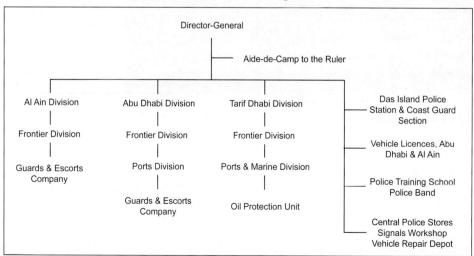

Figure 9: Structure of the Abu Dhabi Police, 1974

Table 5: Leadership of the Abu Dhabi Police

Political head	Executive commander
Ruler: Sheikh Shakhbut bin Sultan Al Nahyan, Ruler of Abu Dhabi (r. 1928-1966) Sheikh Zayed bin Sultan Al Nahyan, Ruler of Abu Dhabi (r. 1966-2004), President of the UAE (1971-2004) **Delegated to:** Major General Sheikh Mubarak bin Mohammed bin Khalifa bin Zayed Al Nahyan, Chairman of Police and Public Security Department, 1966-1971; Abu Dhabi Minister of the Interior, 1971, Federal Minister for the Interior 1971-1990	1957-1959: Staff Sergeant Sheikh Sultan (Commander) 1959-1961: Mr Crosby Stokes (Superintendent/Commandant) 1961-1964: Lieutenant Colonel Bill Edge (Commandant) 1964-1971: Sheikh Mubarak bin Mohammed (Commandant) 1966-1971: Mr A.S. (Stacey) Barham (Deputy Commander) 1971-1974: Hamouda bin Ali Al Dhahiri (Deputy Commander & Federal Minister of State for the Interior) 1974-1975: Mohammed Juma'a Mohammed Al Dhaheri (Director General) 1975-1991: Hamad Saeed Ahmed Al Hassani (Director General)

1967, when its establishment strength was around 600 men, to late 1968 when it numbered 1,000 men.

The growing Abu Dhabi Police force plus the desire of Sheikh Zayed to assist the other Emirates, saw Abu Dhabi provide seconded personnel to train and lead police forces in some other Emirates, as well as providing equipment for them and paying some of their salaries. Abu Dhabi also helped these Emirates by establishing police posts in contentious areas and at border crossing points.

In mid-1971, Sheikh Zayed again reformed Abu Dhabi's government structure, which included establishing Ministries and Ministers. The Abu Dhabi Ministry of the Interior was established with Major General Sheikh Mubarak bin Mohammed becoming Minister of Interior-Abu Dhabi. This Ministry was charged with naturalisation and passport matters, prison affairs, traffic affairs, guarding of oil installations, liaison with Arab and international police directorates, fighting illegal entry of people, drugs and other forbidden substances, and prevention of crime. It oversaw the Abu Dhabi Police, which by this time had an Emirati Deputy Commandant – and effectively, the executive commander of the force–Hamouda bin Ali Al Dhahiri.

Following the formation of the UAE in December 1971, the Federal Ministry of the Interior was established with Major General Sheikh Mubarak bin Mohammed also holding this post. In May 1972, Hamouda bin Ali Al Dhahiri was appointed as the Minister for State for the Interior, in effect the executive interior minister.

In 1973, as part of the move towards greater federalisation of government functions, the Abu Dhabi Government abolished its ministries and ministers, replacing them with Departments/Directorates and Chairmen/Directors-General. In the case of Abu Dhabi Police, in 1974 its formal name became the General Directorate of Police within the Federal Ministry of the Interior, and the Abu Dhabi Police's executive commander now carried the title of Director-General. The first Director-General of Abu Dhabi Police was Mohammed Juma'a Mohammed Al Dhaheri (1974-1975), followed by Hamad Saeed Ahmed Al Hassani (1975-1991).

The 1970s saw a significant expansion of the Abu Dhabi Police as the economy boomed and the population exploded, funded by oil revenues after the 1973 oil price hikes. Police stations were expanded, new equipment like speed radars and CCTV were introduced, and for the first time, women served in the police.

The organisational structure of the Abu Dhabi Police also changed significantly. By 1974 it was structured around three territorial divisions under a General Headquarters which also controlled some critically important, Emirate-wide functions. Each territorial division was responsible for a network of police stations across their territory, and for border control at airports, land crossings or ports. Depending on the location, each division was also responsible for protecting critical infrastructure, including broadcasting facilities and petroleum infrastructure. The three divisions were Abu Dhabi Division, which was responsible for Abu Dhabi Island and the neighbouring mainland and offshore areas including Das Island; Al Ain Division which was responsible for the inland oases area and southern Abu Dhabi Emirate; and Tarif Division on the western coast of the Emirate which was responsible for western Abu Dhabi Emirate and the inshore islands. By 1977, the force was around 2,500 uniformed officers.

6

AJMAN POLICE

Ajman Police was established in February 1967 by the Ruler of Ajman, Sheikh Rashid bin Humaid Al Nuaimi. He appointed his son, Sheikh Abdullah bin Rashid Al Nuaimi, as the force's Commander-in-Chief. When established, plans were for the force to be made up of a Commander, his Deputy, and 10 constables equipped with rifles provided by the TOS. The TOS agreed to loan one NCO as a drill and weapons instructor, as well as providing a Land Rover on delayed repayment terms. Given the Ruler's lack of resources, both the TOS and Dubai Police provided intial training from late 1967. Abu Dhabi also supported the Ajman force's development by training Ajmani police officers and some equipment.

The Ajman Police had grown by mid-1971 to around 80 strong and its vehicle fleet consisted of two small cars. In the force's early years, the bulk of its members were Ajmani. However, with an increase in commercial opportunities in the UAE following the oil boom of 1973, local citizens left the force. Consequently, by 1976, the force had a strong Yemeni presence and its Commandant was Sudanese.

Administratively by the mid-1970s, the Ajman Police force had become a division of the Federal Police however, the Ruler retained considerable control over it.

Table 6: Leadership of the Ajman Police

Political head
Ruler Sheikh Rashid bin Humaid Al Nuaimi (r. 1928-1981)
Delegated to: Sheikh Abdullah bin Rashid Al Nuaimi

Table 7: Dubai Police	
Political head	**Executive commander**
Ruler:	1956-1958: Captain P.H. (Peter) Clayton (Superintendent)
Sheikh Rashid bin Saeed Al Maktoum (r. 1958-1990)	1958-1965: Major P.G. (Peter) Lorimer (Commandant)
Delegated to:	1965-1975: J. (Jack) Briggs, (Commandant)
Sheikh Mohammed bin Rashid Al Maktoum as Head of Police and Public Security	1975-1980: Colonel Abdullah Khalfan Abu Al Houl (Commandant)
	1980-?: Colonel Dahi Khalfan Tamim (Commandant)

7

DUBAI POLICE

The Dubai Police was established in 1956. Up to this point, township security was provided by a Ruler's armed retainers and guards who manned checkpoints and stood guard at key locations, while policing in the hinterland was done by the Trucial Oman Scouts.

In May 1956, the Acting Ruler of Dubai, Sheikh Rashid bin Saeed Al Maktoum, requested help from the British Political Agency to raise a police force in Dubai. The immediate reason for establishing the force was due to increasing lawlessness, with knife-fights and shop-breaking occurring on a large scale. The Ruler nominated his cousin, Sheikh Mohammad bin Hasher Al Maktoum, to take charge of the police, but requested a British officer to be its executive commander. The Ruler asked for a TOS squadron commander, Captain Peter Clayton, who was known to him. The TOS declined to release him from his existing role, but agreed to allow him to volunteer to assist the police in addition to his existing TOS duties.

On 1 July 1956, the Dubai Police held its first muster at Naif Fort, located in the Dubai market (*souk*) with a strength of 15 men. The backbone of the new force was formed from former TOS members and recruits who had attended the TOS Training School. Over the following months Captain Clayton helped to expand, train and organise this force.

Dubai Police faced its first serious test in the aftermath of the October 1956 invasion of Egypt by Israel, and subsequently the intervention by the UK and France, which sought to regain Western control of the Suez Canal after it had been nationalized by Egyptian President Gamal Abdel Nasser. Below is a description of the response by the Dubai Police to unrest in Dubai from British Government records:

During the night of November 5, the Agency received two reports of a proposed strike and demonstrations in Dubai scheduled for the following day, and immediate steps were taken to strengthen public security. A troop of Trucial Oman Scouts moved into positions at the Agency compound in the early hours of November 6 and mobile patrols of the Dubai Police began to tour the town picking up likely malcontents and visiting places of trouble. No strikes or demonstration took place, although an attempt was made, late in the night of November 5, to set fire to the roof of the garage in the compound of the house of the Assistant Political Agent. Guards and a helpful crowd quickly extinguished the fire and very little damage occurred.

At the beginning of 1957, the force's strength had increased to 30, and by then a noticeable decrease in crimes had been reported. That year saw the force grow substantially, with an additional police station being established and plans to establish a 14-man traffic control and riot section, 10-man CID and immigration group, and a 14-man court and administrative group. The force's weapons were 0.303" rifles, Greener shotguns, 0.38" pistols, truncheons and whistles.

In March 1957, Captain Clayton's posting with the TOS ended and thus so did his leadership of the Dubai Police. He was replaced by a professional British police officer, P. G. Lorimer, and became the Dubai Police Commandant (then known as the Superintendent) in July 1957. He was recruited in Britain and administratively became a member of the TOS, although he was not serving then with the British Army.

At this time, a separatist movement in the interior of Oman was underway, with Dubai being a port through which weapons, explosives and supporters passed. To control this flow, Dubai Police started to impose immigration controls. This further improved public security in the town and increased the public's confidence in the police. Its control capability improved further in July 1961 when it started to use a launch to patrol the Dubai creek at night to prevent small boats from smuggling arms etc. in from large vessels anchored

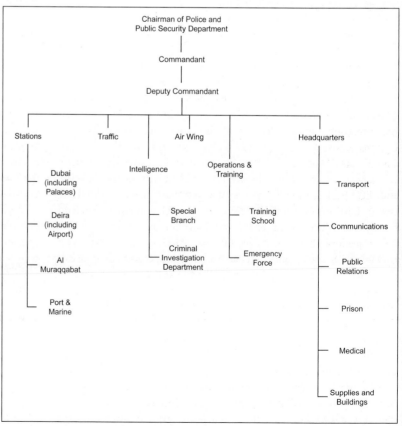

Figure 10: Structure of the Dubai Police, 1974.

Dubai Police badges. Top, the headdress badge comprised of a *dhow*, a wreath with 'Dubai Police' in Arabic script. Centre, rank badges of a general's crossed swords and lieutenant's stars (pips). Bottom, left shoulder rank badge for a major; centre, shoulder title with the Arabic script reading 'Dubai Police'; right, officers' rank insignia. (Courtesy: Cliff Lord)

Early Dubai Police shoulder title. (Courtesy: Cliff Lord)

Major Jack Briggs, Dubai Police Commandant, 1965-1975. His beret is dark green with a golden police force badge. He is wearing a khaki shirt and trousers, with a red lanyard on his left side. Red chevrons were worn by NCOs. The other common uniform worn by police members was olive green army denims. (Courtesy: Dubai Police Museum)

offshore. By this time, the force had grown to 90 men and had also become responsible for immigration and for maintaining a prison. In its early years, the British Government paid for the salaries of the Dubai Police but by the early 1960s, Britain was only paying half of the force's budget and also supported the force by facilitating joint training courses with Dubai Police NCOs and the police forces in Bahrain and Aden.

In May 1965, Major Lorimer left and, as an interim measure, the TOS detached Major Jack Briggs to serve as Commandant of the Dubai Police. Major Briggs was a British policeman with experience in both the Bahrain and Qatar police forces. The TOS had engaged him a few years earlier to form its Police Wing, but this wing had been disbanded when it became obvious it was not going to be accepted within the Emirates' capital towns by their respective Rulers. After serving as the Temporary Commander of the Dubai Police, Major Briggs was asked by the Ruler to become the force's permanent Commandant. He accepted this position and resigned from the TOS. The Dubai Ruler in late 1968 appointed his son, Sheikh Mohammed, as the Head of Police and Public Security, effectively the Minister of Police.

By early 1968, Dubai Police had grown to some 430 personnel. Its command structure consisted of Commandant Briggs, a British Deputy Commandant (Jack K. Humphreys) and two Assistant Commandants. It was structured into the following departments: police stations, traffic, criminal investigation, prosecution and immigration. It was also in the process of forming a Mobile Wing of 200 for anti-riot work and internal security duties, and a Special Branch for security intelligence.

By 1974, the force's total strength was 1,570 including 55 officers. The British presence remained strong and filled the posts of Commandant, Deputy Commandant and three of the five Assistant Commandants who were Foulger, Aubrey and Pugsley (Head of Special Branch). The Dubai Police had access to aircraft via the Police Air Wing which also served Dubai's growing military.

In 1974, the Rulers of the other Emirates agreed to accept control over their police forces by the Federal Ministry of the Interior. However, Dubai declined and kept its police force solely under local control, meaning that the Ruler of Dubai was totally responsible for its budget.

Major changes to the Dubai Police force in the second-half of the 1970s involved its expansion, modernisation and the Emiratisation of positions. Major Briggs was replaced as Commandant in 1975, although he was retained as Adviser and Inspector General to the Ruler until his retirement in 1998.

8

FEDERAL POLICE

Although a UAE Ministry of Interior was formed by 1971, police forces in the early years of the Federation remained Emirate-based entities. The distribution of ministerial posts between the Emirates saw Abu Dhabi control the Interior Ministry, and as Abu Dhabi was the major proponent for greater federalism, it also funded the ministry.

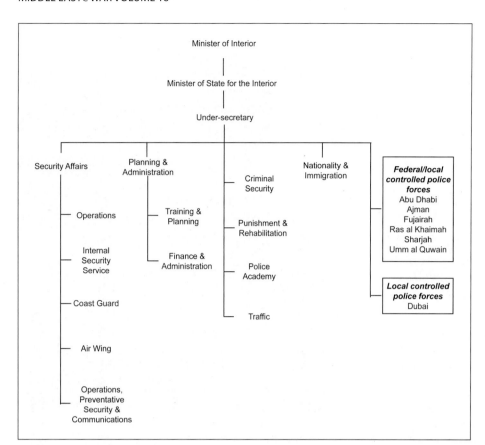

Figure 11: Structure of the Ministry of Interior showing key Federal police functions and relationship with the Police Forces of the Emirates, late 1970s.

Left to right: Sheikh Zayed bin Sultan, Ruler of Abu Dhabi and President of the UAE, and Major General Sheikh Mubarak bin Mohammed bin Khalifa Al Nahyan, UAE Minister of the Interior and Commander of Abu Dhabi Police. In the background is an Emiri Guard officer providing close personnel protection for Sheikh Zayed. (Courtesy: Abu Dhabi Police, mid-1970s)

Table 8: Leadership of the Federal Police	
Political head	**Executive commander**
President: Sheikh Zayed bin Sultan Al Nahyan, Ruler of Abu Dhabi (r. 1966-2004), President of the UAE (1971-2004) **Delegated to:** Major General Sheikh Mubarak bin Mohammed bin Khalifa bin Zayed Al Nahyan, Federal Minister for the Interior, 1971-1990	Early 1970s-1980s: Brigadier General Khalfan Khamis, Under Secretary, Ministry of Interior (effectively Commandant Federal Police)

Major General Sheikh Mubarak bin Mohammed bin Khalifa Al Nahyan, UAE Minister of the Interior, 1971-1990. In addition he was Chairman of the Department of Police and Public Security, 1966-1971; and Abu Dhabi Minister of the Interior, 1971. (Courtesy: Abu Dhabi Police)

Headdress badge of the Ministry of Interior, introduced in 1972. The badge is the UAE Coat of Arms which was also introduced that year. Abu Dhabi, Ajman, Fujairah, Umm Al Quwain and Ras Al Khaimah agreed to the 1973-1974 integration of police forces and replaced their Emirate-specific badges with this badge. (Courtesy: Cliff Lord)

Discussions to integrate all the police forces had been underway for several years, and in December 1973 a meeting was held which proposed a common UAE-wide police budget, financed by Abu Dhabi, and common pay, uniforms and badges across the forces. The Emirates of Fujairah, Umm Al Quwain, Ajman, and Abu Dhabi agreed, with Ras Al Khaimah also joining the arrangement by April 1974. Dubai and Sharjah Police Forces remained independent, with Sharjah subsequently agreeing to unification. In general, the degree of sovereignty an Emirate had over its police force related to its ability to fund the force. The wealthier Emirates of Dubai and, to a lesser degree, Sharjah, had sufficient funds to avoid relying on Abu Dhabi-provided Federal funds for their police force. Accepting Federal funding meant that an Emirate's police force became an expense of Abu Dhabi's budget, and thus gave Abu Dhabi Emirate influence over the force.

To build up Federal police capability, the Ministry of Interior formed its own police. Like the police in each Emirate, the Federal Police had responsibility for not only public security and criminal investigation but also for immigration, maritime patrolling and security intelligence.

By mid-1974, the Ministry of Interior had a total strength of around 1,100 police and civilians, with headquarters in both Sharjah and Abu Dhabi. It was responsible for both land and maritime immigration control in some Emirates. For example, in 1974, it maintained land posts at crossing points at both the Sharjah-Oman and Abu Dhabi-Oman/Saudi Arabia borders, and at Ajman's and Umm Al Quwain's borders. Its Coast Guard patrolled the UAE's coastline, with the exception of areas within Abu Dhabi Emirate which was undertaken by the Abu Dhabi Navy and Abu Dhabi Police Coast Guard. The Coast Guard's headquarters was located in Sharjah, and in 1974 its fleet consisted of four 45ft patrol boats and five to seven small launches. The Coast Guard's bases were small, for example the base at Maaridh in Ras Al Khaimah normally had two or three launches. There was also a Maritime Section in the Ras Al Khaimah Police, at Nakheel, which had one 27ft coastal patrol

Fujairah Police Lieutenant wearing the Fujairah headdress badge and peaked hat, c. 1972-1973. (Courtesy: William Naesmith)

A belt buckle badge of the RAKMF. After 1972, a laurel wreath was introduced around the RAKMF badge. The belt buckle badge is found in white metal and bronze. (Courtesy: Cliff Lord)

launch. The fleet would grow considerably in the late 1970s with the acquisition of fast speed boats and six lightly armed 12m *Dhafeer* class boats which previously were used by Abu Dhabi's naval forces. In the mid-1970s, the Traffic Division of the Ministry of Interior patrolled the roads of the northern Emirates, with the exception of those in Sharjah township and those in Ras Al Khaimah.

In 1973, the Ministry of Interior established the Internal Security Service (also known as the National Security Force) which was a security intelligence service. In 1974, a Federal Law defined its activities as countering espionage and threats to the security of the state and its system of government, as well as preventing damage to the economy. Reports in an Abu Dhabi newspaper of the time stated that its work would be similar to the UK Police's Special Branch and FBI's intelligence branch in the US. Publicly, its establishment was linked with the threat posed by the Popular Front for the Liberation

of Oman and the Arabian Gulf (PFLOAG), the stated aim of which was the seizure of power in Oman and the Emirates as well as the more northerly Gulf States.

The 1970s saw the Ministry of Interior establish its own Air Wing. This was based in Sharjah, and consisted of fixed-wing observation aircraft and helicopters. Its primary coverage area was the northern Emirates, as both Abu Dhabi and Dubai had their own police and military air assets. Federal Prisons maintained by the Federal Police were also established.

9

FUJAIRAH POLICE FORCE

Fujairah was the last Emirate to establish a police force, starting in 1969. Due to its very limited finances, the Fujairah Ruler asked Abu Dhabi to support the formation of his force. This it did by providing a training team from late 1969 to at least 1971. In addition, Abu Dhabi provided weapons, as well as paying the salaries of the officers, and 30 percent of the salaries of the men. By mid-1971, the Fujairah Police strength was 123 men including 2 officers. Its vehicle fleet consisted of six Land Rovers and one Bedford truck. By 1972, the force had grown to 220 men.

Administratively, by the mid-1970s, the force had become a division of the Federal Police, however the Ruler retained significant control over the force.

Table 9: Leadership of the Fujairah Police Force
Political head
Ruler:
Sheikh Mohammed bin Hamad Al Sharqi (1937-1974)
Sheikh Hamad bin Mohammed Al Sharqi (1974-present)

Lieutenant Colonel David Neild, Commander RAKMF, 1971. He is wearing field dress consisting of a khaki shirt and trousers, and a dark green and white chequered *shemagh* with black *agal*. British officers generally wore suede desert boots and the soldiers wore brown leather sandals (chaplis). In the background is a RAKMF Ferret Scout Car. (Courtesy: David Neild)

Lieutenant Colonel David Neild, Commander RAKMF, 1971. He is wearing collar badges which were of the same design as the headdress badge but smaller. The Commander RAKMF wore a green underlay to the collar badges. His silver staybright buttons carry the tower-fort motif. Dress in barracks and parade for officers was an olive green bush jacket with a green lanyard on the right shoulder, and khaki trousers. ORs wore a brick red beret. Brass coloured shoulder titles were worn and had the force's name in Arabic script on them. (Courtesy: David Neild)

10

RAS AL KHAIMAH MOBILE FORCE

Following Britain's 1968 decision to withdraw from the Gulf by 1971, the Ruler of Ras Al Khaimah, Sheikh Saqr bin Muhammad Al Qasimi, was so concerned about the likelihood of a security vacuum and rising threats that he decided to raise his own military. As a result, the Ras Al Khaimah Mobile Force (RAKMF) was formed on 7 July 1969.

The Ruler offered Lieutenant Colonel D.E.G. (David) Neild, a then-serving TOS officer, the position of the force's founding commander if he resigned from the TOS and the British Army. Lieutenant Colonel Neild did so and served in the RAKMF from late 1969 to early 1972. Due to Ras Al Khaimah's limited income, its Ruler in late December 1968 visited Saudi Arabia, to ask for financial support. King Faisal bin Abdulaziz Al Saud agreed to fund the purchase of six Ferret scout cars, twelve 81mm mortars, twelve bazookas, six trucks and six Land Rovers. In August 1969, Saudi Arabia offered additional professional military support in the form of two mechanical and two signal specialists to provide training. The Ruler accepted this offer and Saudi Arabia seconded officers became a feature of the RAKMF for nearly a decade.

Stage one of the RAKMF involved building a force of 120 men, based on four mobile platoons and a medium mortar troop. Initially, recruit training was undertaken by the force's men attending the TOS recruit training depot. Some members of the Ras Al Khaimah Police were also transferred to the RAKMF to help with its development. The Saudi-funded military hardware arrived in 1970. Responsibility for the security of the Emirate was shared between the Ras Al Khaimah Police, which was responsible for town security, and the RAKMF which was the authority for all other areas. The RAKMF's key task was patrolling, which allowed it not only to both build relationships with the mountain tribes but also to intervene in and settle disputes.

By early 1972, when Lieutenant Colonel Neild left the RAKMF, its strength was 300, and it was structured as a mobile infantry squadron (Rifle Squadron), supported by an armoured car troop and mortar troop.

Major Mifta bin Abdulla Al Khatiri, became the force's new commander for a short period until he was replaced by 25-year old Sheikh Sultan bin Saqr Al Qasimi, with Major Mifta serving as Deputy Commander. In mid-1974, the Saudi detachment within the RAKMF had grown to three officers, two NCOs and two technicians. The RAKMF had by this stage a total of 365 personnel. Units included one infantry rifle squadron of five troops, a reconnaissance troop made up of six Ferret scout cars, a mortar troop and a medium machine gun troop. There was also a training school. The Commanding Officer, Deputy Commanding Officer and Officer Commanding the Infantry Squadron were Emiratis; a Saudi major was Signals Officer; and Commander Reconnaissance

Table 10: Leadership of the Ras Al Khaimah Mobile Force	
Political head	**Executive commander**
Ruler:	1969-1972: Lieutenant Colonel D. (David) Neild
Sheikh Saqr bin Muhammad Al Qasimi (r. 1948-2010)	1972-1972: Major Mifta bin Abdulla Al Khatiri
Delegated to:	1972-1976: Sheikh Sultan bin Saqr Al Qasimi
Sheikh Sultan bin Saqr Al Qasimi	

Troop and Supply Officer were Saudi captains.

In 1974, the Ruler recruited Captain (later Major) T. (Tim) Ash to serve as the force's advisor on tribal intelligence. Since the mid-1960s, Captain Ash had served in the TOS and filled the role of Desert Intelligence Officer (DIO). DIO posts were located in Ras Al Khaimah, Al Ain and Mirfa. These officers patrolled their areas collecting tribal intelligence, including Bedouin movements, complaints against Rulers, the levels of water wells, date harvests and environmental conditions. Captain Ash as a DIO worked in the northern Emirates. After 1971 when the TOS became the UDF, he continued to serve until 1974 in the UDF when all of the DIO positions in the UDF were terminated.

Following the unification of the UAE Armed Forces in 1976, RAKMF became Northern Military Region Command.

11
RAS AL KHAIMAH POLICE

In April 1965, the Ruler of Ras Al Khaimah ordered the establishment of a police force. The motivation behind the force was increased insecurity in Ras Al Khaimah town due to a rising population, a desire by the Ruler to provide security rather than relying on the TOS, and optimism that oil would be found and hence the force could be funded. The British supported the formation of the force, with the Officer Commanding TOS Police Wing (Major Jack Briggs) providing administrative and organisational advice, and the TOS supplying 60 0.303" rifles.

The original concept was to establish a force of 60 men stationed in Ras Al Khaimah township and the important areas of Al Araibi, Rams and Al Hamra. By May 1965, 50 men had been recruited and were under training. The force's command structure consisted of Lieutenant Sheikh Khalid bin Saqr Al Qasimi, eldest son of the Ruler of Ras Al Khaimah, the former TOS officer Lieutenant Mifta bin Abdulla Al Khatiri, and a Jordanian sergeant major. The priorities of the force were personal protection for the Ruler, guarding palaces, traffic control and licensing, nightly patrols mostly in the restive northern settlements, duty in the market (*souk*) and criminal investigation. Two Land Rovers were allocated to the force by the Ruler.

Due to a combination of a lack of police experience in the force's leadership, inadequate training and poor conditions, the force suffered from desertions and a lack of recruits in its first year of operation. To address the leadership problem, the Ruler approached the British to find an experienced police officer who could run the force. The British recommended a former British police officer A. T. (Trevor) Bevan, who became Commandant in May 1967. Given the financial problems facing the Ruler and to maintain influence in Ras Al Khaimah, the British agreed to fund the salary of the Commandant, with the Ruler paying for the other personnel. At this time, the force consisted of 120 men and three officers.

Table 11: Leadership of the Ras Al Khaimah Police	
Political head	**Executive commander**
Ruler: Sheikh Saqr bin Muhammad Al Qasimi (r. 1948-2010)	1965-1967: Lieutenant Sheikh Khalid bin Saqr Al Qasimi
	1967-1971: A.T. (Trevor) Bevan, Commandant
	1970s: Sheikh Abdulla bin Mohammad Al Qasimi

While organisation and training improved, funding remained a problem, which meant that personnel were badly paid and ill-equipped. Consequently, retention continued to be a problem, with police members frequently being attracted to serve instead in one of the Emirates' better paying military or police forces. Despite these problems, the force grew to 220 strong by mid-1971. By this time, the force had a police post on one of its islands – Greater Tunb. On 29 November 1971, Iran landed occupying forces on this island. During the assault, 20-year-old Salem Suhail bin Khamis, who led the island's six-man police force, was killed, and another four of its members wounded. Iran has controlled this, and Ras Al Khaimah's other island, Lesser Tunb, to the present.

In 1972, the British Commandant of the RAK Police was replaced by Sheikh Abdulla bin Mohammad Al Qasimi, the younger brother of the Ruler. By the mid-1970s, the force had grown to a total strength of 425 men, including 20 officers. Its headquarters were in the Ruler's old fort, it had eight police posts, with another four planned across the Emirate. In addition to its long-established responsibilities for traffic (including issuing licenses for drivers and vehicles, as well as traffic control), CID, immigration/passport control and Special Branch and Transport/Logistics, the Ras Al Khaimah Police had also established a 25-strong mobile reserve for internal security operations, a Maritime Section with one 27ft coastal patrol launch and a training school. Its small arms now included 0.303" rifles and Spanish 7.62mm CETME rifles (which were the forerunners of the German Heckler & Koch G3 rifle).

Around 1974, the Ruler of Ras Al Khaimah agreed that the Emirate's police would come under the control of the UAE Minister of Interior, which made the Federal Government responsible for funding Ras Al Khaimah's police. This decision was partly driven by a lack of funds, which had seen the salary of a Ras Al Khaimah policeman being a little over half that of the other Emirates police forces. As well as funding the salaries of the Ras Al Khaimah Police, Abu Dhabi also provided personnel for the force. This included an Emirati, Ghobash Ghobash, to head up the immigration department, and two contracted British police advisors, J. Newman and N. Gregor.

Given its limited local policing experience and finances, Ras Al Khaimah also accepted support from Saudi Arabia for its police force. Saudi Arabia provided and paid for a detachment of experienced senior officers who were allocated to Special Branch, Traffic, CID and Transport/Logistics, and also provided training for Ras Al Khaimah police members.

12
SHARJAH NATIONAL GUARD

The Sharjah National Guard (SNG) was a Ruler-controlled force that was formed in 1972. It was established as direct result of the 1972 killing of the Ruler of Sharjah, Sheikh Khalid bin Mohammed Al Qasimi, by his cousin, Sheikh Saqr bin Sultan Al Qasimi. Sheikh Saqr had been the Ruler of Sharjah until 1965 when he was deposed following a loss of support from his family and the British Political Resident, with Sheikh Khalid becoming his successor. On 25 January 1972, Sheikh Saqr and around 20 supporters stormed the Ruler's fort-palace in Sharjah township. During the attack, the Ruler and three palace personnel were killed. Sheikh Saqr proclaimed himself the new Ruler, but was not acknowledged by the UAE Ruling Sheikhs. A combined military operation involving the UDF, ADDF and DDF forced the rebellious sheikh and his followers to surrender.

Subsequently, Sheikh Sultan bin Muhammad Al Qasimi became the Ruler of Sharjah. Recognising that the Ruler and his family were only protected by untrained armed retainers and police, and hence were vulnerable to a small, well-armed and organised adversary, the Ruler agreed to form Sharjah's own military – the SNG.

The principal roles of this force were to ensure internal security and the protection of the Ruler and his close family. Sheikh Abdul Aziz bin Mohammad Al Qasimi, a former TOS captain and, like Sheikh Saqr, a brother of the new Ruler, was given responsibility for overseeing the force's development. Abu Dhabi agreed to fund and equip a force of 14 officers and 230 men. However, it insisted that the force should be known as a national guard, because calling it an armed force would be perceived as contrary to Abu Dhabi's stated policy of bringing the Emirati militaries together, not creating new ones. Sheikh Abdul Aziz contacted Lieutenant Colonel David Neild, whom he had served under in the TOS. Lieutenant Colonel Neild, just-retired as Commander of the Ras Al Khaimah Mobile Force and highly recommended by the Ruler of Ras Al Khaimah, agreed to assist in setting up the SNG. He became the Commander SNG, with Sheikh Abdul Aziz as his 2IC.

In mid-March 1972, the SNG consisted of some 75 former palace guard plus another 55 men who had completed basic training or were awaiting training in Sharjah by instructors loaned by the ADDF. Within a few months of taking command, Lieutenant Colonel Neild had a small, trained 100-man company of light infantry. Within six months, the SNG was operational and had taken full responsibility for the security of the Ruler and his family, with the SNG Commander confident that it could also respond effectively to any civil unrest. This was a remarkable achievement which Lieutenant Colonel Neild attributes to three factors. Firstly, his past experience in establishing a military meant he knew who to approach in Britain to obtain military equipment such as weapons and uniforms. Secondly, he was able to recruit many experienced, well-trained soldiers from the UDF, which allowed serving soldiers to transfer to the SNG. Finally, new facilities did not need to be built as the SNG took over the old TOS facility at Sharjah airport which was renamed the Qasimah Camp. Lieutenant Colonel Neild resigned from the SNG in 1973, by which time the SNG force had grown to 300 men. He handed over command to Sheikh Abdul Aziz, who by then had been promoted to Lieutenant Colonel.

Following the 1973 Tawi Nizwa incident on the Sharjah-Dubai border, the Ruler of Sharjah authorised a doubling of the SNG's manpower. Lieutenant Colonel Sheikh Abdul Aziz also wanted to increase its capabilities, including forming an air wing. However, before this expansion could be actioned, the relationship between the Ruler of Sharjah and Lieutenant Colonel Sheikh Abdul Aziz broke down. This stopped the flow of funds for the SNG, and resulted in Lieutenant Colonel Sheikh Abdul Aziz withdrawing from active involvement in the force. The SNG's effectiveness started to decline as Lieutenant Colonel Sheikh Abdul Aziz had been a driving force in its development. From this point until 1976, the force remained essentially unchanged, being made up of one motorised infantry squadron equipped with light weapons, an armoured car group made up of six Shorland armoured cars, one mortar troop made up of four 81mm mortars, and a Palace Guard of 60 men.

The Sharjah National Guard merged with the Yarmouk Brigade of the UAE Armed Forces in 1976.

SHARJAH NATIONAL GUARD UNIFORM

The SNG wore a khaki jacket, tucked in to khaki trousers. White blancoed 1937 pattern web belt. Brown and white chequered shemagh and black agul. TOS style sandals. Badges of rank and chevrons were British.

Sharjah raised the Amiri Guard in 1984, which lasted until 1990 when integrated into the UAE Armed Forces. The Guard comprised two infantry battalions, an 81mm mortar company, rocket launcher battery, logistics and support companies, and several helicopters and transport planes. Their HQ was in the Merghab area. Khodirah Camp in Dhaid was the training area.

Parade uniform was olive green jacket and trousers, red beret, white belt and anklets, and black boots. SLRs were carried. The cap badge was UAE issue as were rank insignia. A Sharjah flag patch was worn on the right arm.

Table 12: Leadership of the Sharjah National Guard	
Political head	**Executive commander**
Ruler: Dr Sheikh Sultan bin Muhammad Al Qasimi (r. 1972-present)	1972-1973: Lieutenant Colonel D. (David) Neild 1973-1976: Sheikh Abdul Aziz bin Mohammad Al Qasimi

13
SHARJAH POLICE

The origins of the Sharjah Police date to around mid-1966 when the Ruler of Sharjah proposed establishing a 40-strong armed police force. He wanted this force led by his brother, Sheikh Abdul Aziz, who was a Captain in the TOS, but the British convinced him that it would be better to establish the force under an experienced British police officer rather than a military officer. In April 1967, a former British police officer, Mr John I. (Bob) Burns, arrived and became the force's founding Commandant. He was given the rank of Major. He reported to the Sharjah Police Minister (formally known as the Chairman of the Police and Public Security Department), Sheikh Saqr bin Mohammed Al Qaismi who was the brother of the Ruler. The force was formally established on July 1967.

Britain supported the formation of the Sharjah Police because Sharjah was set to become an even more important British military base as additional forces were relocated there following Britain's withdrawal from Aden. Consequently, Britain suggested to the Ruler in November 1966 that the force should consist of two officers, 50 NCOs and constables, and two civilians. Britain also recommended that the force's weapons be 50 Mark IV 0.303" rifles and 15 pistols. Recognising the limited finances of the Ruler, as well as the influence that it would give them, Britain agreed to pay for the Commandant, with the Ruler funding other personnel.

The first batch of 30 police recruits started training under the TOS in September 1967. By February 1968, the force had grown to 57 men with all located in Sharjah township police station. Subsequently, a police station was established in Khor Fakkan, a port town on the Gulf of Oman. Khor Fakkan was a key entry point for foreigners and as such, police work there was heavily focused on immigration which at that time was mostly uncontrolled.

Early Sharjah Police departments included police stations, traffic, and criminal investigation. Around 1970 a Naval Wing was established which focused on controlling immigration, but this role was transferred to the Federal Coast Guard in 1975. The Sharjah

Table 13: Leadership of the Sharjah Police Force	
Political head	**Executive commander**
Ruler:	1967-1971: Major J.I. (John) Burns, Commandant
Sheikh Khalid bin Mohammad Al Qasimi (r. 1965-1972)	1971-1988: Brigadier General Abdullah Al Sari, Commandant
Dr Sheikh Sultan bin Muhammad Al Qasimi (r. 1972-present)	
Delegated to:	
Sheikh Saqr Bin Mohammed Al Qasimi, Chairman of Police and Public Security Department, 1967-1975	

The shoulder title of the Sharjah Police. The Arabic script reads 'Sharjah Police'. (Courtesy: Sharjah Police Museum)

Police also formed a Special Branch which focused on security intelligence, and an Emiri Guard which provided close personal protection and palace guards for the Ruler and senior Royal family members.

Financial constraints on Sharjah in the years immediately after the force was established forced the Ruler of Sharjah to ask Abu Dhabi Emirate to support the force financially. This was agreed to and allowed the force to grow by mid-1971 to some 435 personnel, including four officers and 18 inspectors. This included three British officers. In 1971, the post of Commandant was Emiratised, with Abdullah Juma Majid Al Sari, replacing Major Burns, who became an advisor.

The first commander of Sharjah Police, Major John Burns. He was formerly a Senior Superintendent for Tanganyika Police. (Courtesy: Sharjah Police)

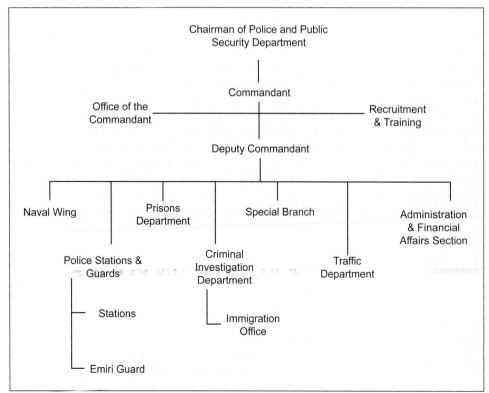

Figure 12: Planned structure for the Sharjah Police, 1967.

In 1972 oil was discovered in Sharjah's waters, which led to a huge increase in the state's revenue. One of the consequences of this discovery was that it allowed Sharjah to significantly expand and modernise its police. By 1974, Sharjah Police's strength was 1,050 personnel. It was structured into Sharjah Town, CID, Traffic and Administration departments, as well as a Special Branch, Drug Squad, a 120-man Oilfield Guard on Abu Musa Island and a newly formed Mobile Emergency Force of some 120 men designated for riot control. All reported to the Commandant, with the exception of Special Branch which reported directly to the Police Minister. The last of the three British expatriates in the force had left by the end of

1973. In 1974, Jordan provided a police team of one officer and four staff sergeants to assist in training.

By the end of the 1970s, the force was structured into four Departments – (1) Management of Guards and Stations, which consisted of 11 police stations in Sharjah town and the surrounding area plus the Emiri Guard; (2) Security Affairs, which consisted of CID, communications, driver and vehicle licencing, and traffic police and rescue services; (3) Personnel and Finance, which included transport, workshops and supplies; and (4) Khor Fakkan Department, which provided policing services in the enclave.

The main light weapon of the Sharjah Police was modernised AK-47 (AKM) assault rifles. Since 1972, it had also been equipped with Shorland armoured cars.

14

UMM AL QUWAIN NATIONAL GUARD

In 1975, the Ruler of Umm Al Quwain, Sheikh Rashid Bin Ahmed Al Mualla, issued a decree forming the Umm Al Quwain National Guard. Its headquarters was at Umm Al Quwain Camp, while the training facility and shooting range were in the Mehtheb area. The force's initial strength was about 180 men, structured into infantry and support companies, and an armoured squadron. Its equipment included 10 Scorpion light tanks, twelve 106mm recoilless rifle mounted in vehicles, and four 81mm mortars. The force appears to have been manned mainly by Pakistanis and officered by ex-patriates.

Early in the existence of the UAQNG the normal khaki uniform of shirt and long trousers was worn along with a *shemagh* of white with red leaves and a black *agal*. A gold coloured cap badge was worn, depicting a cannon, similar in appearance to the police cap badge but with a different scroll and base. Buttons were gold in colour, showing the cannon device of the National Guard. When merged into the UAE Armed Forces, the new camouflage uniform had a camouflage epaulet with black embroidered rank and the Arabic script showing Umm Al Quwain National Guard. A brown beret was worn. A chrome belt buckle had the cap badge affixed in the centre.

The Umm Al Quwain National Guard merged with the UAE Armed Forces in 1976.

The Ruler of Sharjah, Sheikh Khalid bin Mohammed Al Qasimi, inspecting a Sharjah Police parade, late 1960s. The marching ORs are wearing white 1937 pattern webbing with holster for a revolver, and those at attention have Romanian AKM rifles. (Courtesy: Sharjah Police)

Sharjah Sheikh's Bodyguard. (Courtesy: Tony Ford)

Table 14: Umm Al Quwain National Guard
Political head
Ruler:
Sheikh Ahmad bin Rashid Al Mu'alla (r. 1929-1981)
Delegated to:
Colonel Sheikh Saud bin Rashid Al Mu'alla

15

UMM AL QUWAIN POLICE

The Ruler of Umm Al Quwain, Sheikh Ahmad bin Rashid Al Mu'alla, decided to establish a police force in 1967. At that time, the emirate had just several thousand inhabitants. The force's original structure was a Commander, Deputy and 20 constables equipped with rifles. Its vehicle fleet consisted of just one Land Rover. As the British supported the Rulers of the northern Emirates in developing

Umm Al Quwain National Guard shoulder title.(Courtesy: Umm Al Quwain Police Museum)

Umm Al Quwain National Guard gold coloured cap badge. (Courtesy: Umm Al Quwain Police Museum)

Umm Al Quwain National Guard collar badge as worn on khaki-red shirt. (Courtesy: Umm Al Quwain Police Museum)

Umm Al Quwain National Guard camouflage rank epaulet. Although shown on a later style of uniform, this design was in use from the mid-1970s. (Authors' collection)

The belt buckle of the Umm Al Quwain Police. The Arabic script reads 'Umm Al Quwain Police'. (Courtesy: Umm Al Quwain Police Museum)

UAE chrome police belt buckle. (Courtesy: Umm Al Quwain Police Museum)

their own police forces, the TOS provided rifles and agreed to loan one NCO as a drill and weapons instructor. Dubai Police also provided NCOs to assist with training, which started in late 1967. From early 1969, Abu Dhabi became the principal provider. It seconded one of its police officers, Mohamad Juma, as the force's new commander, and another as its second-in-command. Abu Dhabi also provided equipment, such as establishing radio-telephone communication between Umm Al Quwain and the Abu Dhabi Police. By mid-1971, the Umm Al Quwain Police was 82 strong, including 2 officers, and was equipped with some 70 0.303" rifles.

The early police uniform comprised a khaki shirt and long trousers with chrome buttons. A chrome belt buckle was worn with the police badge device engraved on it, along with a black beret and lanyard. Shoulder titles were worn with the inscription 'Umm Al Quwain Police' on them, and later replaced with UAE police titles.

Administratively, by the mid-1970s, the force had become a

The aluminium headdress badge of the Umm Al Quwain Police Force. The badge consists of a cannon encircled with laurel leaves and the Arabic script under it reads 'Umm Al Quwain Police'. The badge was issued in gold and silver coloured metal, though it appears there was no significance attached to which colour was worn. The badge of the Umm Al Quwain National Guard was similar but the shape of the scroll was different, as was the script. (Courtesy: Umm Al Quwain National Museum)

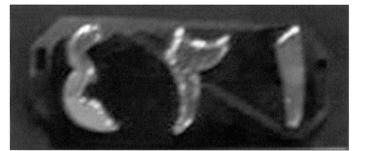

The personal number of a member of the Umm Al Quwain Police. The number was worn over the breast. In Arabic, personal numbers are called military numbers rather than police numbers. (Courtesy: Umm Al Quwain National Museum)

A single rank pip is shown along with a shoulder title stating Umm Al Quwain Police. (Courtesy: Umm Al Quwain National Museum)

Umm Al Quwain Police 2nd type, chrome shoulder title. The script reads 'Umm Al Quwain Police'. (Courtesy: Umm Al Quwain National Museum)

Union Police white metal title. (Courtesy: Umm Al Quwain Police Museum)

In 1973–1974, the Umm Al Quwain adopted the Federal Minister of the Interior's uniform and badges. (Courtesy: Umm Al Quwain Police Museum):

division of the Federal Police, however the Ruler of Umm Al Quwain retained substantial control over the force.

Table 15: Leadership of the Umm Al Quwain Police	
Political head	**Executive commander**
Ruler: Sheikh Ahmad bin Rashid Al Mu'alla (r. 1929-1981) **Delegated to:** Colonel Sheikh Saud bin Rashid Al Mu'alla	1967-?: Mohamad Juma, Commander

UDF Dodge Power Wagons in the Liwa region, c. 1973. A large canvas provides shade between the two vehicles. (Courtesy: William Naesmyth)

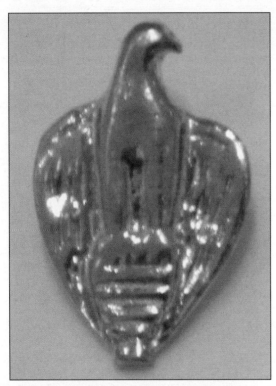

UDF major's rank insignia, 1971-1975. (Courtesy: Nick Weekes)

UDF shoulder title, 1971-1975. The Arabic reads "Union Defence Force". The Signal Squadron had a blue plastic underlay under the shoulder title. (Courtesy: Cliff Lord)

UDF headdress badge, 1971-1975. The Arabic script under the crossed daggers reads 'Union Defence Force'. The silver headdress badge was worn by all ranks on a black *agal* securing the red and chequered *shemagh*. The manufactured version of the UDF badge was in staybrite metal but most officers wore solid silver versions which they procured locally. (Courtesy: Eddie Parks)

16

UNION DEFENCE FORCE/ FEDERAL ARMED FORCE

The UAE came into existence on 2 December 1971 following the expiration of the British-Trucial States treaties at midnight the day before. The emirates were no longer British Protected States, and the UAE was now responsible for its own external defence as well as its foreign relations. As such, the British no longer wanted to maintain its military – the Trucial Oman Scouts (TOS), a British locally raised Arab military force led by British officers and NCOs. At this time, the TOS consisted of 1,500 personnel based at five camps across the Emirates.

In the lead up to its 1971 departure, Britain had recommended to the Emirates' Rulers that they needed to form a union for self-protection and establish a union military, rather than maintaining individual Emirate forces. Britain advocated that the nucleus of the

new union's military should be the TOS and the individual Emirate forces should be integrated into it.

On 21 December 1971, the TOS was formally disestablished and all of its members were discharged. The following day, a UAE law came into effect that established the Union Defence Force (UDF). The law stated that the UDF was under the supervision of

UDF radio operator in a Series 3 109 Land Rover, Fitted for Radio, along with a UDF soldier holding a SLR, early 1970s. (Courtesy: Dubai Federation Museum)

its air wing was small and limited to transport and communication aircraft. It was logical to build a unified force around the ADDF rather than the UDF for obvious military reasons, and also for political reasons. Thirdly, the internal peace-keeping role that the UDF inherited from the TOS was becoming obsolete as this responsibility was being taken over by the various Emirati police forces, including the new gendarmerie-type Federal Police, as they improved their capabilities. This meant that it made little sense to expand the UDF based around an internal security mission. Finally, there was a strong perception that the UDF was still very much a British force as all the most senior posts were held by British officers.

In 1973, the UAE Rulers commenced talks on the unification of the various military forces in the UAE. While a decision on national unification was postponed, the UAE Minister of Defence issued a decree renaming the UDF the Federal Armed Force (FAF) in 1974. To reflect the force's federal nature, a new device and headdress badge based on the UAE Coat of Arms was introduced. (This would also become the headdress badge of the UAE Armed Forces after it was formed in 1976). A new flag was also developed, this being a

the Federal Minister of Defence, Sheikh Mohammed bin Rashid Al Maktoum, the then-22 year-old, third son of the UAE Prime Minister and Ruler of Dubai, Sheikh Rashid bin Saeed Al Maktoum.

All members of the TOS were invited to join the UDF. Almost 99 percent of the TOS re-enlisted with the UDF. Most of the serving British officers and NCOs also volunteered to stay on, becoming seconded officers. Day one saw virtually no change with a force identical in structure and personnel to the TOS.

While Britain had hoped that the UDF would become the basis for the UAE's federal army, this did not occur for four main reasons. Firstly, money was not provided initially to allow the force to grow and re-equip. Being a federal force, it was funded by the federal government. As Abu Dhabi was the principal source of funding for the federal government, it prioritised funding the Abu Dhabi Defence Force over the UDF. Secondly, over time, it became increasingly impractical for the UAE to unify its forces around the UDF. Abu Dhabi's ADDF was much larger and better equipped than the UDF and this gap increased over time. In early 1974, the UDF had around 3,000 men while the ADDF was over four times that size with 13,000 men. In addition, the ADDF was a full spectrum force with a superior air and sea wing, while the UDF had no sea wing and

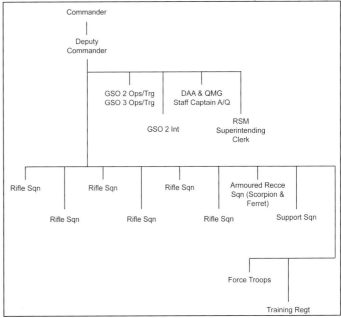

Figure 13: Federal Armed Force, 1975.

UDF Ceremonial Quarter Guard on Parade. At the right can be seen a horse of the Mounted Troop with its white saddle cloth and red border, c. 1972-1973. (Courtesy: William Naesmith)

A detachment of E Squadron UDF on patrol armed with a SLR and Sterling sub machine guns. They are wearing field desert boots and Pakistan made 1944 pattern derivative webbing, c. 1973. (Courtesy: William Naesmyth)

Table 16: Leadership of the Union Defence Force/Federal Armed Force	
UAE President	**Commander UDF/FAF**
Sheikh Zayed bin Sultan Al Nahyan, Ruler of Abu Dhabi (r. 1966-2004), President of the UAE (1971-2004)	1971-1974: Colonel H.E.R. (Roy) Watson
	1974-1974: Lieutenant Colonel K. (Ken) Wilson
Delegated to:	1974-1976: Lieutenant Colonel R.H. (Richard) Robinson
Sheikh Mohammed bin Rashid Al Maktoum as Minister of Defence (1971-present)	

Senior officers of the FAF, c. 1975. They are wearing the sand coloured beret which replaced the *shemagh* for normal daily wear when the force was renamed the FAF. The beret carries the FAF headdress badge which replaced the UDF badge. Members of the Military Police Squadron wore red berets and those in the Armoured Squadron wore black. In the photo, all the lanyards worn are red, which signifies a member of a combat unit, except for the one in the centre which is green, signifying a non-combatant officer (e.g. an education officer). Back row, right to left: Lieutenant Colonel R. Robinson; Major Michael Jones, General Staff Officer Grade 2 Staff Duties; unknown; unknown; Lieutenant Colonel Saleh Nasser GSO 1 Operations. Front row: unknown. (Courtesy: R. Robinson)

red flag that had the UAE national flag in the canton (i.e. the top quarter nearest the pole, making the flag look like a UAE version of the British Red Ensign). The implementation to the force's new name, devices, badges etc appears to have been inconsistent, resulting in the force still being referred as the UDF in official documents and on base signage, and using old UDF elements until all Emirati forces were unified in 1976.

As well as a new name, the force was given a new role in 1973. No longer was its mission to be internal security. Instead, the UDF/FAF's primary mission was to defend the external borders of the six northern Emirates. This required the force to become a regular infantry, brigade-sized, battle group. The plan to build this force, approved in late 1973, required three years, with some of the needed changes already well underway.

A first step was to expand the force by forming a sixth Rifle Squadron; this was named 'E' Squadron. Another was to form an armoured reconnaissance force; by the end of 1973, the FAF had 18 Ferret Scout cars and 10 Scorpion light tanks. A heavy weapons troop would be added to some rifle squadrons and the force's support squadron would be up-armed. New weapons planned for purchase included 24 GMPGs, 50 LMGs, six Carl Gustav 84mm anti-tank recoilless rifles, 25 60mm mortars, and six 81mm mortars. Training was also changed to reflect defensive warfare and the tactics of a modern military force. By 1975 the force had an establishment strength of 3,250 men. By this time, a rifle squadron consisted of about 220 all ranks, which was larger than its British equivalent. Each squadron was formed of three rifle troops, a motor transport group and a squadron HQ troop which included a 15-man signal

section. The squadron vehicles consisted of 22 Land Rovers, three Bedford 4-ton trucks and a water bowser.

As of 1975 the FAF comprised six infantry squadrons, one armoured squadron, a support squadron, a training squadron and Force Troops. Support Squadron (once known as Support Group) was responsible for the Force's 81mm mortars (mounted in Dodge Power Wagons) and held some Browning heavy machine guns in store. Not shown in the organisation chart (Figure 13 on page 49) is that the FAF also had a small parachutist unit, a boys' squadron, the Air Wing, plus a Signal Squadron which formed part of Force Troops alongside HQ Squadron, Transport Squadron, Medical Squadron, Ordnance Squadron, Workshop Squadron, Works Squadron (i.e. Engineer Construction Squadron), Education Squadron and Guard Squadron.

The Air Wing was raised in early 1972, with its first commander being the contracted British officer, Squadron Leader (later Lieutenant Colonel) P.K. (Peter) Wooldridge. Its first aircraft were three AB 206B Jet Ranger light observation helicopters provided by the ADDF which had recently acquired Alouette light helicopters as replacements. It would have been logical to base the helicopters at Sharjah where the British had left behind helicopter landing pads, workshops and facilities, but because the Ruler of Sharjah demanded rent, the Minister of Defence decided to base the helicopters at Dubai Airport. The April 1974 expansion plans for the Air Wing consisted of purchasing four Bell 205A-1 troop lift helicopters (first arrived in June 1975) and two Pilatus PC-6 Porter single-engine short take-off and landing (STOL) utility aircraft.

The final stage in developing the FAF into a battle group was to reorganise the force into two combat regiments. This involved forming two groups of three squadrons into two regiments and restructuring the Force HQ into a Brigade HQ. The Training Squadron was also expanded to become a Training Regiment.

In May 1976, the process of unifying the various Emirati military forces into the UAE Armed Forces started. This would see the Sharjah National Guard becoming integrated with the FAF, and the new force being re-designated as the Yarmouk Brigade under the command of the General Headquarters (GHQ) Abu Dhabi.

17
UNITED ARAB EMIRATES ARMED FORCES

Between 1971 when the UAE was formed and 1976, multiple military forces existed in the country. There was one federally-controlled military – the Union Defence Force/Federal Armed Force (1971-1976) – and four Ruler-controlled forces – the Abu Dhabi Defence Force (1965-1976), Ras Al Khaimah Mobile Force (1968-1976), Dubai Defence Force (1971-1976), and Sharjah National Guard (1972-1976). Technically there was a sixth, the Umm Al Quwain National Guard formed in 1976, however, as this was very small and had no notable operational capabilities, it is not considered a 'force' in a military sense.

After years of discussing the need to amalgamate all these militaries into just one Federally-controlled force, on 6 May 1976, the UAE's highest authority, the Supreme Council, passed a decree which authorised this. This date marks the founding of the UAE Armed Forces, and is celebrated annually to the present day. The process of unification of the forces can be seen in Figure 14.

The military headquarters of the UAE Armed Forces was located in Abu Dhabi city, with Abu Dhabi Emirate providing the vast majority of the force's funds. To allay concerns held by the other Emirates over Abu Dhabi's influence on this force, as well as to respect the symbolic and security value that the individual forces had for the other Rulers, the initial structure of the UAE Armed Forces was based on regional commands, and thus essentially continued the previous Emirate-based control arrangements. Three land-based regional commands were introduced – Western Military Command (formerly Abu Dhabi Defence Force), Central Military Command (formerly Dubai Defence Force) and the Northern Military Command (formerly Ras Al Khaimah Mobile Force). In addition, another land formation was established in Sharjah, known as the Al Yarmouk Brigade (formerly the Federal Armed Force into which was integrated the Sharjah National Guard). Each of these formations were commanded by a son of the respective Rulers in which the Command or Brigade was based. The UAE Air Force and UAE Navy continued as national forces, although the Central Military Command maintained a separate air force known as the Dubai Air Wing. The helicopter-based Air Wing of the Federal Armed Force became the Air Wing of the Federal Ministry of Interior, and was primarily responsible for providing search and rescue and policing services in the northern Emirates, as the more southerly emirates of Dubai and Abu Dhabi had their own police air wings. The comparative size of the force elements of the UAE Armed Forces in 1976 (Table 17) shows that Abu Dhabi's Western Military Command was larger than all the other land-forces combined, and that it maintained the most technologically advanced force. The table also shows that while the land forces were commanded by Emiratis, the Air Force and Navy remained commanded by non-

Emirati seconded officers.

The chain of command for the UAE Armed Forces following the 1976 unification was from the Supreme Commander, who was Sheikh Zayed bin Sultan Al Nahyan, President of the UAE, to the Deputy Supreme Commander, Sheikh Khalifa bin Zayed, who was the oldest son of Sheikh Zayed (Table 18). Reporting to him was the professional head of the military, the Chief of Staff. The first Chief of Staff was a seconded Jordanian officer, and it was only in 1980 that an Emirati filled this post. The structure strongly reflects the British headquarters structure of the period.

The introduction of geographic commands, while retaining the pre-unification local control arrangements, did little to improve lack of uniformity in standards, methods and equipment across the forces, nor did it reduce the duplication of forces and facilities. To address these problems, in January 1978 Sheikh Zayed unilaterally issued several decrees to restructure the military. One decree cancelled the regional commands, except for Dubai's Central Military Command, and introduced a fully unified command structure which gave GHQ full control over all land, sea and air forces. The decree also created the post of Commander-in-Chief as the immediate superior to the Chief of Staff. Sheikh Zayed filled this post by promoting his then 23-year old second son, Colonel Sheikh Sultan bin Zayed, to Brigadier General. The land forces of the regional command were restructured into brigades, with each headed by a Lieutenant Colonel or Colonel reporting directly to GHQ.

The reorganisation decisions – and particularly its lack of consultation – greatly irritated the Rulers of Dubai and Ras Al Khaimah in particular. They viewed the reorganisation as a way of centralising military power under Abu Dhabi's control, and thus limiting their autonomy and ability to protect themselves. Consequently, both Rulers pulled their forces out of the new command structure, and re-established their own local control.

After a period of tension in early 1979, a political compromise was worked out which saw, in October of that year, the Ruler of Ras Al Khaimah agreeing to place his force (now known as 2nd Brigade) under the command of GHQ. Dubai, with its greater financial resources, did not agree to reintegrate its force back into the UAE Armed Forces at this time, and this would only occur in the late 1990s.

Figure 15 shows the reorganised force structure as of 1980. It reflects the reintegration of Ras Al Khaimah's forces back into the structure, but the ongoing separation of Dubai's forces from GHQ. It also shows that the Ministry of Defence was only responsible for Central Military Command forces.

LAND FORCES

The 1978 restructuring of the UAE Armed Forces saw the regional commands being reorganised into brigades. Central Military Command became 1st Brigade (although it was referred to as Central Military Command into the late 1990s), Northern Command became 2nd Brigade (named Al Badr Brigade), and Western Command became 4th Brigade (named Al Dhafra Brigade). The Al Yarmouk Brigade became 3rd Brigade. As of 1978, 1st, 2nd and 3rd Brigades were essentially motorised light infantry forces supported by armoured reconnaissance elements. The units making up 4th Brigade had, since 1975, been receiving both armoured personnel carriers and infantry fighting vehicle, meaning that by 1978, 4th Brigade was well on its way to becoming a fully mechanised infantry force.

At this time, there were also three other non-infantry combat

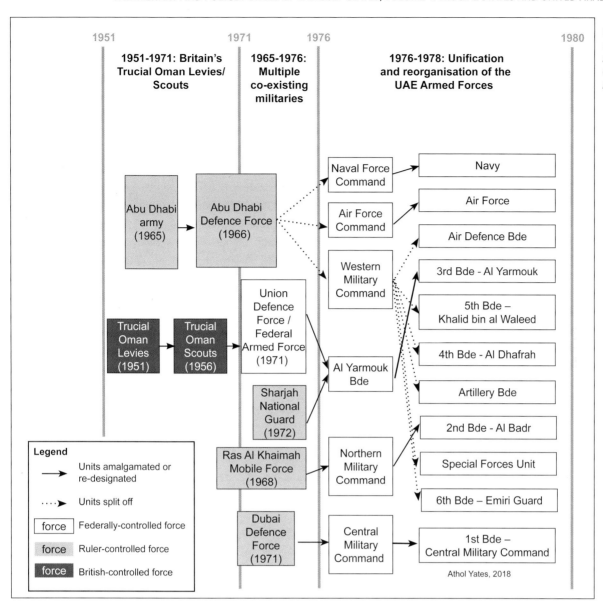

Figure 14: Antecedent militaries of the UAE Armed Forces and its evolution. (Diagram by Athol Yates)

Table 17: Force elements of the UAE Armed Forces immediately following the 1976 unification

Force	Main constitute force	Head-quarters location	Professional military commander	Key force characteristics
Army-Western Military Command	ADDF	Abu Dhabi	Colonel Sheikh Sultan bin Zayed Al Nahyan (2nd son of the Ruler)	15,000 establishment strength, one armoured brigade, two infantry brigades, a light Emiri Guard brigade, an artillery regiment, Defence Signal and a training regiment.
Army–Central Military Command	DDF	Dubai	Colonel Sheikh Ahmed bin Rashid Al Maktoum (4th son of the Ruler)	2,600 establishment strength, an armoured car squadron, three infantry squadrons, signal squadron, a support squadron, and Emiri Guard.
Army–Northern Military Command	RAKMF	Ras Al Khaimah	Colonel Sheikh Sultan bin Saqr Al Qasimi (son of the Ruler)	700 establishment strength, three infantry companies, and a support company which included armoured cars.
Al Yarmouk Brigade	UDF/FAF	Sharjah	Colonel Shaikh Humaid Abdulla Al Qasimi (cousin of the Ruler)	4,600 establishment strength, two combat infantry regiments, a training regiment, and armoured, signal and support squadrons.
Navy	ADDF Sea Wing	Abu Dhabi	Colonel Nabil Madhwar (Egyptian seconded officer)	300-400 establishment strength, fleet of six 110ft Vosper, three 56ft and six 40ft patrol boats (based in Abu Dhabi).
Air Force	ADDF Air Wing, UDF/FAF Air Wing	Abu Dhabi	Brigadier General Ghulam Haider (Pakistani seconded officer)	550-1,200 establishment strength, fleet of Mirage 5EAD and Mirage 5AD fighters, 5 fighter/attack aircraft, helicopter squadron and communication flight (all Abu Dhabi), Hawker Hunter squadron (based at Sharjah).

Table 18: Leadership of the UAE Armed Forces, 1977

Political head	Executive commander
UAE President and Supreme Commander:	**Chief of Staff**
Sheikh Zayed bin Sultan Al Nahyan, Ruler of Abu Dhabi (r. 1966-2004), President of the UAE (1971-2004)	1976-1980: Major General Awadh Mohammed Al Khalidi
	1980-1981: Brigadier General Mohammed Said
Delegated to:	**Regional Command structure (1976-1978)**
Deputy Supreme Commander (1976-2004): Sheikh Khalifa bin Zayed Al Nahyan	Western Military Command: Colonel Sheikh Sultan bin Zayed Al Nahyan
Commander-in-Chief (1978-1982): Brigadier General Sheikh Sultan bin Zayed Al Nahyan	Central Military Command: Colonel Sheikh Ahmed bin Rashid Al Maktoum
	Northern Military Command: Colonel Sheikh Sultan bin Saqr Al Qasimi
	Al Yarmouk Brigade, Colonel Sheikh Humaid Abdulla Al Qasimi
Minister of Defence (1971-present): Sheikh Mohammed bin Rashid Al Maktoum	**Reorganised UAE Armed Forces structure (1978-1980s)**
	1st Brigade (Central Military Command), Colonel Sheikh Ahmed bin Rashid Al Maktoum
	2nd Brigade (Al Badr infantry): Colonel Sheikh Sultan bin Saqr Al Qasimi
	3rd Brigade (Al Yarmouk infantry): Colonel Sheikh Humaid Abdulla Al Qasimi
	4th Brigade (Al Dhafrah mechanised Infantry): Colonel Ahmed Salim Ali?
	5th Brigade (Khalid bin Al Waleed armoured): Colonel Khamis Saeed?
	6th Brigade (Emiri Guard): Brigadier General Khalfan Mattar Saeed Al Rumaithi
	Artillery Brigade
	Commander Air Force
	Mid-1970s-1977: Brigadier General Ghulam Haider (Pakistani seconded officer)
	1977-1980: Brigadier General Jamal Ahmad Khan (Pakistani seconded officer)
	Commander Navy
	1975-1983: Brigadier General Mohammed Nabil Madhwar (Egypt seconded officer)

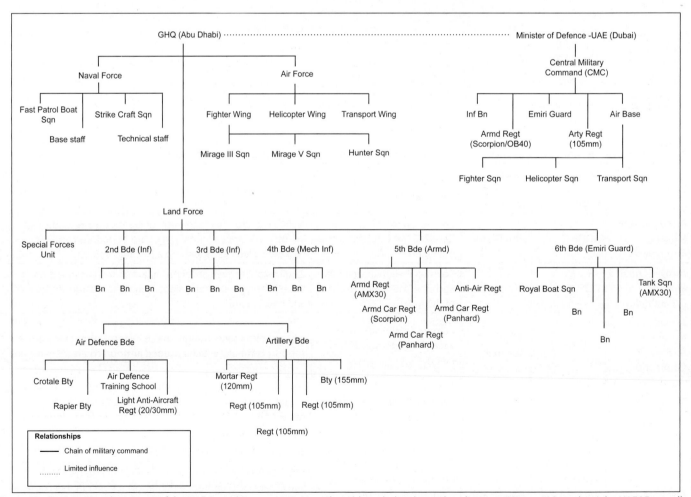

Figure 15: Organisational structure of the UAE Armed Forces, 1980. Note that although the above chart lists one 'Mirage III Squadron', the UAEAF actually never operated Mirage IIIs: British intelligence reports citing 'Mirage IIIs' actually referred to the squadron equipped with Mirage 5EDA interceptors (equipped with an improved variant of the avionics suite from the Mirage IIIE). (Courtesy: The National Archives, UK)

The headdress badge of the Central Military Command, 1976-1978. After 1978, the Central Military Command, technically became known as 1st Brigade, however, locally it continued to be referred to as Central Military Command until the late 1990s. (Courtesy: Cliff Lord)

The plaid brooch of the Pipe Band of the Central Military Command. (Courtesy: Cliff Lord)

brigades – all formerly part of Western Command. There was also a 5th Armoured Brigade, named Khalid bin Al Waleed Brigade, an Artillery Brigade and an Air Defence Brigade. From the mid-1970s onwards, all three started to receive large quantities of new equipment.

The Armoured Brigade's capabilities increased significantly with the arrival of 90 AML 60/90 wheeled armoured cars between 1976 and 1978. The Artillery Brigade received both towed L-118 105mm and Model-56 105mm guns, and AMX-Mk-F3 155mm self-propelled guns in the second half of the 1970s. The Artillery Brigade also had a 120mm mortar regiment.

As of 1978, the Air Defence Brigade consisted of light air defence guns. It would grow over the following few years to include a battery each of Rapier and Crotale surface-to-air missiles. This brigade would become merged with the Air Force in 1987.

The Central Military Command also grew significantly in the second half of the 1970s. In 1977, CMC's approximate strength was 3,500 men. By 1980, it was about double this size. In 1976, it had an armoured regiment made up of wheeled light and medium armoured cars and tracked armoured reconnaissance vehicles, and by 1981 it would start to receive OF-40 Italian main battle tanks. In 1976, its artillery consisted of one artillery squadron with 105mm light guns plus another with 20mm anti-aircraft guns; by 1980, it had started to receive RBS-70 surface-to-air missile systems.

Land Forces also included special forces. Their history starts in November 1971 with the formation of the ADDF's Tariq bin Ziyad Group. This group was the renamed 9 Squadron, also known as Force HQ Defence Squadron, which had been formed in early 1971. The Tariq bin Ziyad Group was raised to be an elite, physically fit, infantry fighting force. To mark its difference from the other infantry forces, its members wore a camouflage uniform plus green beret, both unique in the ADDF at that time. The name change reflected a change in its image from an infantry squadron to a commando unit which could fight collectively or in small elements undertaking daring raids. During one particular military parade, an announcer shouted out "Here come the Desert Wolves", an unofficial nick-name that the group kept among themselves. The founding OC of both 9 Squadron and Tariq bin Ziyad Group was Major T.D. (Tim)

Cooper, a British contract officer. He was succeeded in 1973 by another British contract officer, Major A. (Andrew) Baker, and by early 1974, the first national (Major Ahmed Salem) was appointed OC for the Group.

In its early years, the Group's training focused on fitness and advanced infantry tactics. In 1973, a Special Forces school or wing was established in Al Ain which offered Special Forces training for officers and NCOs who had completed commando training. The instructors were Jordanian. Later in the 1970s, parachute training was introduced.

From mid to late-1970s, the Group expanded through the amalgamation of various special forces and parachute units. By the start of the 1980s, the UAE special operations forces consisted of some 850 personnel structured into one battalion, with camps in Abu Dhabi, Al Ain and Sharjah. A second battalion was planned.

AIR FORCE
When the first air force of the Emirates was established in 1968, its role was to support land forces through ground attack, observation and provision of transport aircraft. Since the early 1970s, the air force's roles have been broadened to those of a modern air force – that is, air space awareness and control, bombing, and support to land and maritime forces. As of 1976, the UAE Air Force consisted of four BN-2 Islanders, one DHC-4 Caribou, 12 Hawker Hunters fighter/ground attack aircraft, five SA 316B Alouette III light helicopters, and three SA 330 Puma helicopters, and a number of Mirages. The Mirages were delivered in two batches. The first consisted of ten 5AD fighter-bombers and two 5RAD reconnaissance aircraft (delivered 1973-1974), and the second of two 5AD fighter-bombers, one 5RAD reconnaissance aircraft, one 5DAD (two seater) trainer and fourteen 5EAD radar-equipped fighter-bombers (delivered 1976-1977).

Central Military Command also had an air force known as the Dubai Air Wing. As of 1976, its military aircraft consisted of three Bell 206/OH-58 light helicopters, one Cessna 182 Skylane light aircraft, two Bell 205/UH-1D helicopters, one SIAI-Marchetti SF.260W Warrior military trainer, an Aeritalia G.222 medium-sized STOL military transport aircraft, and six Macchi single-seat MB-326KD ground attack aircraft, later supplemented by two two-seat MB-326LD advanced jet trainers.

The ADAF originally acquired four de Havilland Canada DHC-4 transports. A fifth was purchased to replace one lost in an accident. This aircraft – serial 301 – was photographed in November 1975. (Courtesy: Tom Cooper)

The replacement DHC-4 – serial number 305 – was the only one known to have worn a camouflage pattern (probably in form of dark earth applied atop of yellow sand). (Courtesy: Albert Grandolini)

The third Hunter FGA.Mk 76 of what was originally the 'Hunter Squadron', and later the I Shaheen Squadron ADAF, as seen in August 1972. (Courtesy: Albert Grandolini)

The first of three FR.Mk 76A single-seat reconnaissance fighters (serials 708-710) of the ADAF, as seen in the mid-1970s. (Courtesy: Albert Grandolini)

The first of two Hunter T.Mk 77 two-seat conversion trainers (serials 711-712) acquired by the ADAF in the period 1969-1971. Like all single-seaters, they were originally in light stone and dark brown on upper surfaces and sides, and light admiralty grey on undersurfaces. (Courtesy: Albert Grandolini)

In the second half of the 1970s, the UAE Air Force increased its ground attack capabilities by acquiring HOT second-generation long-range anti-tank missiles for its SA-342 Gazelle helicopters.

NAVY

Following the 1976 unification of the Emirati militaries, the UAE Navy consisted of six 110ft, three 56ft and six 40ft patrol boats, plus a number of smaller and support vessels. The Navy's main naval base had moved in 1975 from the side of Abu Dhabi Island, where access was restricted during low tide, to a new naval base at Abu Dhabi port. By this time, the Navy also had forward operating bases on Das Island (then the centre of offshore oil and gas export activities), at Dohat Al Quwaisat on the far west of Abu Dhabi's coast, and at Khor Fakkan on the Gulf of Oman on the UAE's east coast.

In 1975, the UAE Navy had a strength of some 400 personnel, the majority of whom were expatriates. While the first few years of Abu Dhabi's naval force, contracted British officers dominated the officer corps, by 1976, they had mostly been replaced by Egyptians and Pakistani seconded officers. Ratings were mostly Omani, with technical posts primarily filled by Pakistanis.

Throughout the 1970s there was an emphasis on increasing the number of Emiratis in naval officer posts. While the Navy could provide short courses and on-the-job training, it did not have the resources or capabilities to deliver more substantial education and training. Consequently, naval cadet and officer training was primarily done in foreign countries, as was much specialist training of ratings. Britain was a key source of education and by the late 1970s, the UAE

Navy commenced a program to train the bulk of its Emirati officers at Royal Navy establishments. This education, plus the fact that the UAE Navy was established by British naval officers, resulted in the UAE Navy's doctrine reflecting that of Britain.

In 1977, the responsibility for maritime border law enforcement was transferred from the UAE Navy to the newly formed UAE Coast Guard which was controlled by the Ministry of Interior. To provide the Coast Guard's nucleus of vessels, the Navy gave the new organisation all six of its 12m *Dhafeer* class patrol boats. With the creation of the Coast Guard, three separate forces were now responsible for the maritime domain – the maritime units of the local and Federal police forces, the Coast Guard (primarily operating in the northern Emirates), and the Navy (primarily responsible for all of Abu Dhabi's non-port waters plus all the other Emirates' offshore waters). These arrangements continued until the early 2000s.

The need to up-arm the Navy became pressing when the navies of both Iran and Saudi Arabia expanded greatly in the 1970s. Given the UAE's limited manpower and naval skills, obtaining large conventional warships was impractical. Thus, around 1977, the UAE ordered a new type of vessel – the fast attack craft (FAC). These vessels were a radical naval innovation that enabled small vessels fitted with surface-to-surface missiles to destroy conventional warships. FACs can be deployed individually to shadow hostile vessels and enforce blockades, or in swarms which enabled them to threaten even the largest capital ships: for example, in 1967 a Soviet-built Egyptian FAC sank an Israeli destroyer. Since then, FACs have been purchased by multiple Middle Eastern nations due to their

Through the early 1970s, Dubai developed a strong preference for Italian-made aircraft: when the military and police forces of all seven emirates were united, its air wing took over the responsibility for training. Correspondingly, a total of 6 MB-326KD advanced trainers (visible here) and 2 MB-326LD basic trainers were acquired from Aermacchi in Italy. (Courtesy: Tom Cooper)

Links to Italy resulted in Dubai contributing to the establishment of the United Arab Emirates' Union Air Force through the acquisition of a single Aeritalia G.222 general-purpose transport. The aircraft entered service in November 1977. (Courtesy: Tom Cooper)

A left-hand view of the sole G.222. Notable is the short-lived roundel consisting of the air force's crest on the white field, with outside field in red and including the inscription 'Union Air Force' applied in black and in Arabic on the top, and in white and in English on the bottom. (Courtesy: Albert Grandolini)

low cost (excluding weapon systems), easy maintenance and small manpower requirements. The first of these six 45m FACs (*Bani Yas* class) vessels arrived in 1980. They were each equipped with four MM.40 Exocet anti-ship missiles which could target vessels over 70km away (providing the attacking craft has the ability to locate the enemy at this range). The Exocets represented a major leap in capabilities as the previous heaviest naval weapon then in the Navy's arsenal was the 20mm cannon, fitted to the *Kawkab* class boats, an ineffective gun against warships. Unlike later FACs, the *Bani Yas* class had no air defence capabilities or electronic countermeasures, relying on the vessels' high speed and manoeuvrability to avoid being destroyed by aircraft. Other limitations of the early FACs were that they lacked both the seakeeping to operate in higher sea states and multi-day endurance due to their small size and cramped quarters.

18
SIGNIFICANT FOREIGN OPERATIONS, 1951-1980

In January 1972, following a rebellion in Sharjah, the separate militaries of the UAE came together for the first time to collectively undertake a military operation. This was seen as an early watershed in achieving unity in the newly formed country, given historic tensions between certain Rulers. Below is a detailed description of the operation. The information is derived from the Commander UDF's report of the rebellion, written the day after its end, and a first-hand report written by Major C.G.B.H. (Cameron) Mackie, OC C Squadron, who led the tactical response until he was wounded.

Table 19: Significant Foreign Operations

Date	Units involved	Description
1952-1955	TOL	Buraimi Crisis: Following the Saudi occupation of the Omani parts of Buraimi in 1952, the TOL (supported by other British forces and tribal elements) first contained, and then in 1955 forcefully expelled the Saudis.
1957-1959	TOS	TOS elements operated in Oman to support the Sultan of Oman's forces and other British forces in their efforts to defeat a separatist movement.
1973-1974	ADDF	Following a request from the Sultan of Oman in 1973, Abu Dhabi sent two ADDF infantry squadrons to the city of Sohar in northern Oman, which allowed Sohar's Omani gendarmerie unit to deploy to fight rebels in Dhofar in southern Oman. The squadrons were based in Sohar from October 1973 to January 1974, and again from November 1974 to April 1975.
1973	ADDF	During the 1973 Arab-Israel War (6 to 25 October 1973), the ADDF Air Wing's Caribous served as air ambulances in Jordan.
1977-1979	UAE Armed Forces	UAE Armed Forces participated in the Arab Deterrent Force in Lebanon which sought to maintain the internal security of Lebanon at the beginning of the outbreak of the civil war. The 750-man UAE contribution involved five rotations of troops.

A beautiful study of the second out of three SA.330C Pumas (serials 111-113) acquired by the ADAF. (Courtesy: Albert Grandolini)

The ADAF acquired a total of five SA.316B Alouette helicopters in the early 1970s. They received serial numbers 101-105, and were painted in the same colours as the Pumas. (Courtesy: Albert Grandolini)

The rebellion started around 1400 hrs on 24 January 1972 when a group of armed supporters of Sheikh Saqr bin Sultan Al Qasimi stormed the Sharjah Fort in which the Ruler of Sharjah, Sheikh Khalid bin Mohammed Al Qasimi, resided. Sheikh Saqr bin Sultan had ruled Sharjah from 1951 to 1965 before being deposed and exiled. He had returned secretly to Sharjah, assembled a small force and stormed the fort. Shots were fired and unbeknownst to those outside the fort, the Ruler was killed, along with two guards and two staff.

The Commandant of Sharjah Police, Major J.I. (Bob) Burns, phoned Colonel Watson, Commander UDF at the UDF headquarters in Murqaab Camp and requested that UDF troops be sent to the fort. Within 20 minutes, the Commander UDF, plus Major Mackie OC C Squadron, a small number of C Squadron

troops, and Major Budd, UDF Intelligence Officer, left for Sharjah Fort. Arriving on site around 1500 hrs, they found that the fort was firmly in the hands of Sheikh Saqr bin Sultan, and there was sporadic ongoing fire between the fort and Sheikh Saqr bin Mohammed, the brother of the Ruler, who was firing from the roof of his house, some 300 yards away, with an LMG. Faced with this situation, the Commander UDF immediately instructed that the UDF Intelligence Officer should return to the UDF's Murqaab Camp to open the operations room, that the remainder of C Squadron be sent immediately to the fort area, and that one troop from each of D Squadron (based at Manama in Ajman) and X Squadron (based at Ham Ham in Ras Al Khaimah) move to Sharjah.

By 1600 hrs, the UDF forces at Sharjah Fort consisted of 34 men from C Squadron, as the rest were on Eid leave and could not

Acquired on advice from Pakistani personnel – which served in Abu Dhabi starting from 1972, following a corresponding agreement between Sheikh Zayd and President Bhutto of Pakistan – Mirage 5ADs became the first supersonic fighter-bombers of the ADAF. (Tom Cooper Collection)

be recalled quickly. The Sharjah Police had also brought up their Shorland armoured patrol cars, which are lightly armoured vehicles based on the Land Rover Series IIA chassis and are designed to carry a MMG. However, the cars arrived without either arms or trained crews.

The number of rebels in the fort was estimated as between eight and 20 men, armed with small arms, LMGs and grenades. Based on this assessment, the Commander UDF decided to attack the fort. He ordered OC C Squadron to plan the attack, which was to involve an LMG team providing covering fire for the UDF's main force towards to the fort's main gate. This would be dangerous as reaching the fort wall required crossing about 200 yards of open ground with very little cover. The police armoured car was to force open the gate, with additional covering fire from the rooftop of Sheikh Saqr bin Mohammed's residence. Before the attack was launched, several Sharjah sheikhs asked for more time to allow those in the fort to be contacted by telephone and given the chance to surrender. Consequently, a delay was ordered. It was during this time that it appears contact was made with the Defence Minister, Sheikh Mohammed bin Rashid. At 1715 hrs, he authorised the attack. However, once again before the attack could be launched the Sharjah sheikhs requested a further delay so that contact with those in the fort could again be attempted. "On his own initiative" at 1745 hrs, the Commander UDF ordered the attack to commence.

Starting at 1750 hrs, under the direct command of OC C Squadron, UDF troops started moving forward supported by handful of Bedouin guard and fire from the rooftop of Sheikh Saqr bin Mohammed's house, as planned. The police armoured car, now driven by the Police Commandant, hit the main gate which burst open. Immediately, the OC C Squadron charged through the gate to be confronted by heavy fire. He was shot in the leg but made it back to the gate where his troops were waiting for his signal to enter. Realising that the defending force was bigger than expected and that there would be high causalities if an attempt to rush the fort proceeded, it was decided not to press the attack. Given the injury, OC C Squadron second-in-command, Captain G. (Gene) Kerr, took over command of C Squadron troops.

At 1815 hrs, the situation for the UDF became more complicated as the Commander UDF received intelligence that an armed force was on its way to support the rebels. Fortunately, very soon after this, additional troops from both D and X Squadrons arrived. These troops went to provide rear protection for the operation, as well as to support C Squadron coverage of the fort. With night approaching, the Commander UDF instructed Major Ken Wilson, OC X

Squadron to reconnoitre the fort.

By this stage, Sheikh Zayed had ordered the ADDF to support the operation; an infantry squadron was flown into Dubai Airport and a Saladin armoured car squadron was driven from Abu Dhabi. Dubai also provided two troops from the DDF, totalling 35 men. A planning meeting was held at 2135 hrs at the UDF operations room in Murqaab Camp. The key players there were the Defence Minster, Commander UDF and the Director Military Liaison Officer (Brigadier General De Butts). Rather than undertaking a night attack against a well-armed and positioned enemy which would result in high casualties, it was decided that the best way to end the rebellion was through a "show of strength and demonstration of military superiority." It was hoped this would convince the defenders that their rebellion was doomed to failure and they would surrender. Rather than assaulting the fort with troops, the plan involved placing breaching explosives along the fort's wall during the night and at 0500 hrs next morning (25 January) these would be detonated and Shaikh Saqr bin Sultan called upon to surrender. If he did not, the ADDF's Saladin armoured cars, supported by the infantry, would concentrate fire for 2 minutes at one part of the fort (so as to limit damage) and then again call for his surrender. If this did not work, the sequence would be repeated.

By 0430 hrs, the explosive charges were laid, with the UDF troops in place close to the fort and the Saladins ready for immediate deployment. The operation was protected by ADDF and DDF troops who provided the outer cordon. The Defence Minister and other leaders were at the tactical operations centre near the fort. From there, the Minister contacted Sheikh Saqr bin Sultan by telephone and requested he both surrender and produce the Ruler unharmed. Being told by Sheikh Saqr bin Sultan that the Ruler was already dead, the Minister hung up and called both Sheikhs Zayed and Rashid for consultation. The planned detonation of the explosive charges was suspended. At 0530 hrs, the Minster again called Sheikh Saqr bin Sultan and convinced him to surrender. He agreed and he emerged from the fort with five other ringleaders. Shortly afterwards, groups of his followers, totalling around 20 also came out and surrendered.

Subsequently, the fort was searched by Commander UDF, the OC X Squadron, UDF troops, and the Commandant of Sharjah Police for any remaining supporters as well as for the dead. Once this was done, the site was handed over to the police.

19

UAE MILITARY AND POLICE RANKS

The rank structure of Emirati military and police forces is based on the British Army, and as seen below is nearly identical. While the TOL/TOS also used British Army ranks, the Arabic terms for them were slightly different from Emirati forces. The TOL/TOS ranks and their Arabic equivalent were Commandant (Qa'id), Lieutenant-Colonel (Qaimaqam), Major (Muqaddam), Captain (Rais), Lieutenant (Mulazim), 2nd Lieutenant (Mulazim thani), Warrant Officer Class I (Wakil Al qwa), Warrant Officer Class II (Wakil Al sarie), Staff-sergeant (Naqeeb), Sergeant (Shawish), Corporal (Areef), Lance-corporal (Jundi awal) and Private (Jundi).

Ranks	Arabic	Transliterated Arabic	British Army
General	فريق أول	Feriq awwal	General
Lieutenant General	فريق	Feriq	Lieutenant General
Major General	اللواء	Lewa	Major General
Brigadier General	عميد	Amid	Brigadier
Colonel	عقيد	Aqid	Colonel
Lieutenant Colonel	مقدم	Muqaddam	Lieutenant Colonel
Major	رائد	Ra'id	Major
Captain	نقيب	Naqib	Captain
1st Lieutenant	ملازم أول	Mulazim awwal	Lieutenant
Lieutenant	ملازم	Mulazim	2nd Lieutenant
Warrant Officer Class I	وكيل أول مساعد (military) أول (police)	Wakeel awwal (military) mosa'ad awwal (police)	Warrant Officer 1
Warrant Officer Class II	وكيل (military) مساعد (police)	Wakeel (military) mosa'ad (police)	Warrant Officer 2
Staff Sergeant / 1st Sergeant	رقيب أول	Raqib awwal	Staff Sergeant
Sergeant	رقيب	Raqib	Sergeant
Corporal 1st class (only military)	أول عريف	Areef awwal	
Corporal	عريف	Areef	Corporal
Lance Corporal / Policeman 1st class	جندي أول (military) شرطي أول (police)	Jundi awwal (military)–Shurti awwal (police)	Lance Corporal
Private / Policeman	جُنْد (military) شُرْطّي (police)	Jundi (military) Shurti (police)	Private / Constable

BIBLIOGRAPHY

Interviews and correspondence with veterans of the forces, former UK and Emirates' civil servants and historians: G. Barnett (TOS), M. Butler (ADDF and Abu Dhabi Special Branch), T. D. Cooper (ADDF Land Forces), H. A. Culley (UDF/FAF 1973-1975), M. Curtis (TOS), F. Ford (TOS), V. Gervais (Emirates Diplomatic Academy), D. J. Gregory (ADDF Sea Wing), R. Hitchcock (ADDF), B. McCombe (ADDF), A. MacDonald, W. Naesmith (UDF), D. Neild (RAKMF and SNG), H. Nicklin (TOS), J. Onley, H. Pugh, O. Raw-Rees, R. Robinson (UDF/FAF and Al Yarmouk Brigade), A. Rossiter (Khalifa University), R. Sheridan (ADDF Air Wing), D. H. A. Sievwright (UDF/FAF), K. Steel (TOS/DDF), M. Stockwell (TOS/DDF), P. Sweet (ADDF Sea Wing), M. Timmis (TOS), N. C. F. Weekes (UDF/FAF), J. J. Williams (DDF), Catherine Lord, Aaron Fox, Gordon A Mackinlay and Tim Ash (TOS, UDF/FAF, RAKMF).

Museums and institutions including Abu Dhabi Police, Dubai Police Museum, Imperial War Museum, Middle East Centre Archive, St Antony's College at Oxford, National Archives of the UAE, National Archives of the UK, Royal Signals Museum, Royal Society for Asian Affairs, Sharjah Police Museum and the Umm Al Quwain National Museum.

The key files used at The National Archives of the UK were: CAB 147/97, DEFE 11/880, DEFE 68/397, FCO 371/179929, FCO 371/74718, FCO 8/1241, FCO 8/1245, FCO 8/1255, FCO 8/1814, FCO 8/2134, FCO 8/2371, FCO 8/2430, FCO 8/2660, FCO 8/2897, FCO 8/3101, FCO 8/3105, FCO 8/3925, FCO 8/4385, FCO 8/4973, FCO 8/5459, FCO 8/5468, FCO 8/6172, FCO 8/6176, FCO 8/910, FO 1016/736, FO 371/114589, FO 371/114680, FO 371/120627, FO 371/157038, FO 371/18549, FO 371/185548, FO 371/185551, FO 371/75018, FO 371/82175, PREM 15/2153, WO 32/1643, WO 331/11, WO 337/11, WO 337/13, WO 337/15, WO 337/15.

A Short History of the Royal Air Force Regiment (Ramsgate: R.A.F. Regiment Fund, 1974).

Al Abed, Ibrahim, Paula Vine, and Abdullah Al Jabali, *Chronicle of Progress: 25 Years of Development in the United Arab Emirates* (London: Trident Press, 1996).

Al Dhaheri, Nasser, *Roll of Honour The Armed Forces of the United Arab Emirates* (UAE Directorate of Morale Guidance, The Armed Forces of the UAE, 2006).

Al-Mazrouei, N.S., *The UAE and Saudi Arabia Border Disputes and International Relations in the Gulf* (London: I.B. Tauris, Limited, 2016).

Al Moalla, Sheikh Majid Abdulla, *Analysis of the United Arab Emirates' National Security* (PhD, Durham University, 2017).

Al Ulama, Hesam Mohammed Jalil Sultan, *The Federal Boundaries of the United Arab Emirates* (PhD, University of Durham, 1994).

Barratt, R.H., *British Influence on Arab Military Forces in the Gulf: The Trucial Oman Scouts*, (MA, American University of Beirut, 1972).

Bradshaw, T., 'The Hand of Glubb: The Origins of the Trucial Oman Scouts, 1948-1956', *Middle Eastern Studies* 53, no. 4 (Jul 2017), pp 656-672.

Burdett, A. (ed)., "Annual Records of the Gulf" (Archives Edition, various editions).

Cawston, A., and M. Curtis, *Arabian Days Memoirs of Two Trucial Oman Scouts* (Chandlers Ford: Cedar Colour Printing, 2010).

Clayton, P., *Two Alpha Lima: The First Ten Years of the Trucial Oman Levies and Trucial Oman Scouts 1950 to 1960* (Cambridge: Janus Publishing Company, 1999).

Curtis, M., 'On Secondment with the Trucial Oman Scouts 1966-1968', (Liwa: *Journal of the National Center for Documentation & Research*, no. December Volume 2, Number :4 (December 2010).

Davidson, C.M. *The United Arab Emirates: A Study in Survival* (Lynne Rienner Publishers, 2005).

de Butts, Col F.M., *Now the Dust Has Settled: Memories of War and Peace, 1939-1994* (Padstow: Tabb House, 1995).

Edwards, F., *The Gaysh: A History of the Aden Protectorate Levies 1927-61 and the Federal Regular Army of South Arabia 1961-1967* (Solihull: Helion & Company, 2004).

Faraj, Essa Juma, *Environmental Influences on The External Relations of The United Arab Emirates*, (MA, Carleton University, Ottawa, 1973).

Friedman, B., "From Union (ʿittihād) to United (Muttahida): The United Arab Emirates, a Success Born of Failure", *Middle Eastern Studies* 53, no. 1 (2017/01/02 2017).

Gervais, V., *Du Petrole a l'Armee. Strategies de construction de l'Etat aux Emirats Arabes Unis* (Paris: IRSEM, 2011).

Hawley, Sir D., *The Trucial States* (London: Allen & Unwin, 1970).

Heard-Bey, Frauke., From *Trucial States to United Arab Emirates : A Society in Transition* (London: Longman, 1982).

Henderson, E., *This Strange Eventful History: Memoirs of Earlier Days in the UAE and the Sultanate of Oman*, (Dubai: Motivate Publishing, 1993).

Horniblow, P., *Oil, Sand and Politics: Memoirs of a Middle East Doctor, Mercenary and Mountaineer* (Kendal: Hayloft, 2003).

Illustrated History of Military Ranks, United Arab Emirates Armed Forces 1951-2013, (Abu Dhabi: UAE Armed Forces Museum and Military History Center, 2013).

Iqbal, Ali, and Peter Hellyer, "The UAE in World War Two: The War at Sea", *Tribulus* 25 (2017).

Iqbal, Ali, Peter Hellyer and Laurence Garey, "The UAE in World War Two: A Forgotten Fatal Air Crash in Sharjah", *Tribulus* 25 (2017).

Joyce, M., *Ruling Shaikhs and Her Majesty's Government, 1960-1969* (London: Taylor & Francis, 2004).

Khalifa, A.M., *The United Arab Emirates: Unity in Fragmentation* (Boulder: Westview Press, 1979).

Kneen, J.M., and D.J. Sutton, *Craftsmen of the Army: The Story of the Royal Electrical and Mechanical Engineers Vol II 1969-1992* (Barnsley: Pen & Sword Books Limited, 1997).

Lee, David, *Flight from the Middle East: A History of the Royal Air Force in the Arabian Peninsula and Adjacent Territories, 1945-1972* (London: Her Majesty's Stationery Office, 1981).

Long, D.E. and B. Reich, B. (ed), Anthony, John Duke and John A. Hearty, *Eastern Arabian States: Kuwait, Bahrain, Qatar, the United Arab Emirates, and Oman, In the Government and Politics of the Middle East and North Africa* (Boulder: Westview Press, 1980).

Lord, C., and D. Birtles, *The Armed Forces of Aden 1839-1967* (Solihull: Helion, 2000).

Lord, C., and G. Watson, *The Royal Corps of Signals: Unit Histories of the Corps (1920-2001) and Its Antecedents* (Solihull: Helion, 2014).

Louis, W.R., S.R. Ashton, and University of London, *Institute of Commonwealth Studies, East of Suez and the Commonwealth 1964-1971* (London: Her Majesty's Stationery Office, 2004).

Lunt, J.D., *Imperial Sunset: Frontier Soldiering in the 20th Century* (London: Macdonald Futura, 1981).

Maitra, J. *Zayed, From Challenges to Union,* (Center for Documentation & Research, 2007).

Mann, M., *The Trucial Oman Scouts: The Story of a Bedouin Force* (Norwich: Michael Russell, 1994).

Mawby, S., *British Policy in Aden and the Protectorates 1955-67: Last Outpost of a Middle East Empire* (London: Taylor & Francis, 2006).

Morton, M.Q., *Buraimi: The Struggle for Power, Influence and Oil in Arabia* (London: I. B. Tauris, 2013).

Naylor, M., *Among Friends: The Scots Guards 1956-1993* (Barnsley: Pen and Sword, 1995).

Neild, David, *A Soldier in Arabia* (Surbiton: Medina Publishing, 2016).

Oliver, K.M., *Through Adversity: The History of the Royal Air Force Regiment, 1942-1992* (Rushden: Forces & Corporate, 1997).

Onley, J., *Britain and the Gulf Shaikhdoms, 1820-1971: The Politics of Protection* (Dohar: Center for International and Regional Studies, Georgetown University School of Foreign Service in Qatar, 2009).

Orders and Medals of the United Arab Emirates Armed Forces 1951-2008, (Abu Dhabi: UAE Armed Forces Museum and Military History Center, 2013).

Peterson, J., *Defending Arabia,* (London: Croom Helm, 1986).

Pivka, Otto von, *Armies of the Middle East* (United Kingdom: Patrick Stephens, 1979).

Porter, R. "The Trucial Oman Scouts (TOS) 1951-1971." *The Bulletin: Journal of the Military Historical Society 41,* no. 163 (1991).

Priestland, J., (ed.), *The Buraimi Dispute: Contemporary Documents 1950-1961,* Volume 5: 1954-1955 (Farnham Common: Archive Editions Limited, 1992).

Rashid, Noor Ali, *Sheikh Mohammed: Life and Times* (Dubai: Motivate Publishing, no date).

Rossiter, A. "Strength in Unity: The Road to the Integrated UAE Armed Forces", *Liwa: Journal of the National Archives 7,* no. 13 (2015).

Rossiter, A., *Britain and the Development of Professional Security Forces in the Gulf Arab States, 1921-1971: Local Forces and Informal Empire* (Exeter: University of Exeter 2014).

Stanley-Price, N., *Imperial Outpost in the Gulf: The Airfield at Sharjah (UAE) 1932-1952* (Leicester: Book Guild Publishing, 2012).

The Journey Proceeds 1957-2017 (Abu Dhabi: Abu Dhabi Police, 2017).

The UAE Armed Forces History and Missions (Abu Dhabi: UAE Armed Forces Museum and Military History Center, 2011)

Walcot, Tom. "The Trucial Oman Scouts 1955 to 1971: An Overview", *Asian Affairs 37,* no. 1 (2006/03/01 2006) pp. 17-30.

Ward, T., and H. Nicklin (eds.), *Are You the Man* (United Kingdom: Trucial Oman Scouts Association, 2014).

Warwick, N.W.M., *In Every Place: The RAF Armoured Cars in the Middle East 1921-1953* (Rushden: Forces & Corporate Publishing 2014).

With United Strength: *H.H. Shaikh Zayid Bin Sultan Al Nahyan, the Leader and the Nation* (Abu Dhabi: Emirates Center for Strategic Studies and Research, 2004).

Yates, Athol, "Western Expatriates in the UAE Armed Forces, 1964–2015", *Journal of Arabian Studies 6,* no. 2 (2016).

Yates, Athol, *The evolution of the UAE Armed Forces* (Solihull: Helion, forthcoming).

Abu Dhabi Police, *The Journey Proceeds 1957–2017* (Abu Dhabi: 2017)

Abu Dhabi Police, *Abu Dhabi Police: Fifty Years of Progress 1957–2007* (Abu Dhabi: 2007

AUTHORS' NOTE

This book details the military and police forces of the Emirates of Abu Dhabi, Dubai, Ras Al Khaimah, Sharjah, Umm Al Quwain, Ajman and Fujairah. Historically, these Emirates were collectively known as the Trucial States, which in 1971 federated to form the United Arab Emirates (UAE). From the 1892 to 1971, treaties between the Rulers of each Emirate and Britain had made all the Trucial States British protected states. This meant that Britain was responsible for the external defence and foreign affairs of these states, but internally, each Emirate retained sovereignty.

This book starts from 1951 which was when the first professional military force was raised in the Trucial States – the British-controlled Trucial Oman Levies. Before this, Rulers kept small forces of armed retainers and guards. Efforts to raise a Ruler-controlled force started in 1954, with the first enduring force, the Dubai Police, being established in 1956. In 1965, the first Ruler-controlled military was established – the Abu Dhabi Defence Force. By the time the UAE was formed, all seven Emirates had established their own police forces with three also forming military forces.

Sheikh Zayed bin Sultan Al Nahyan, Ruler of Abu Dhabi from 1966 and UAE President from 1971, had always argued for federalising both the Emirate-based police and military forces, and by the second-half of the 1970s, significant steps were made towards this goal. These included bringing a number of police forces under the control of the Federal Ministry of Interior in 1973-1974, and unifying the various militaries into the UAE Armed Forces in 1976, although there were subsequent setbacks to federalisation efforts. By the end of the 1970s, all the major security institutions seen in the UAE today had been established.

While there is very limited, publicly available, accurate and detailed information on the military and police forces of the UAE, we have been able to build a comprehensive and accurate picture of developments through scores of interviews with veterans and experts, visits to archives in both the UAE and the UK, and discussions with military historians. It has been a privilege to help to record the contribution made by so many in creating safety, stability and security for the UAE.

We wish to thank all those that contributed to the writing of this book, without whom it would not have been so comprehensive. In particular, we appreciate the great contributions made to the research and editing of the book by Sheikh Zayed bin Hamad Al Nahyan, Rachid Kerkab, Jacinta Nelligan, Peter Hellyer, Khaled Al Shehhi, Ahmed Khamis, Musabbeh Khalfan Al Ghaithi, Ahmed Khalfan Al Ghaithi, Robin Hitchcock, Catherine Lord, Aaron Fox, G.A. Mackinlay and Eddie Parks.

Athol Yates and Cliff Lord, 2018